IN SEARCH OF

Robinson Crusoe

IN SEARCH OF

Robinson Crusoe

Daisuke Takahashi

English Translation by Juliet Winters Carpenter

Cooper Square Press

All photos courtesy of the author, except where noted.

First Cooper Square Press edition 2002

This Cooper Square Press hardcover edition of *In Search of Robinson Crusoe* is an original publication; a Japanese-language edition without the eighth chapter and postscript and with thirteen fewer photographs was published by Shinchosha in Tokyo in 1999. This English-language edition is published by arrangement with the author.

Published by Cooper Square Press,
A Member of the Rowman & Littlefield Publishing Group
200 Park Avenue South
Suite 1109
New York, NY 10003
www.coopersquarepress.com

Distributed by National Book Network

Library of Congress Cataloging-in-Publication Data

Takahashi, Daisuke, 1966–
    [Robinson Kuråusåo o sagashite. English]
    In search of Robinson Crusoe / Daisuke Takahashi ; translated by Juliet Winters Carpenter—1st Cooper Square Press ed.
        p. cm.
"A Japanese edition without the eighth chapter and postscript and with thirteen fewer photographs was published by Shinchosha in Tokyo in 1999"—T.p. verso.
Includes index.
    ISBN 0-8154-1200-2 (cloth: alk. paper)
1. Selkirk, Alexander, 1676–1721.   2. Survival after airplane accidents, shipwrecks, etc.—Juan Fernândez Islands.   3. Defoe, Daniel, 1661?–1731. Robinson Crusoe—Sources.   4. Takahashi, Daisuke, 1966—Journeys.   I. Title.
    G530.S42 T3513   2002
    996.1'8—dc21   2002004433

Printed in the United States of America

⊗™ The paper used in this publication meets the minimum requirements of American National Standard for Information Sciences—Permanence of Paper for Printed Library Materials, ANSI/NISO Z39.48-1992.

"*From this moment I began to conclude in my mind that it was possible for me to be more happy in this forsaken, solitary condition than it was probable I should ever have been in any other particular state in the world; and with this thought I was going to give thanks to God for bringing me to this place.*"

—Daniel Defoe, *The Life and Strange Surprising Adventures of Robinson Crusoe*

For My Mother

Contents

Maps

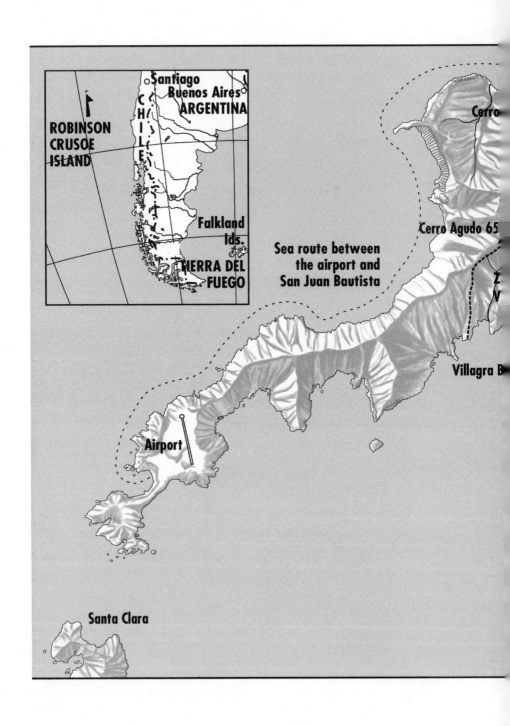

ROBINSON
CRUSOE
ISLAND

Santiago
Buenos Aires
ARGENTINA

CHILE

Falkland
Ids.

TIERRA DEL
FUEGO

Cerro

Cerro Agudo 65

Sea route between
the airport and
San Juan Bautista

Villagra B

Airport

Santa Clara

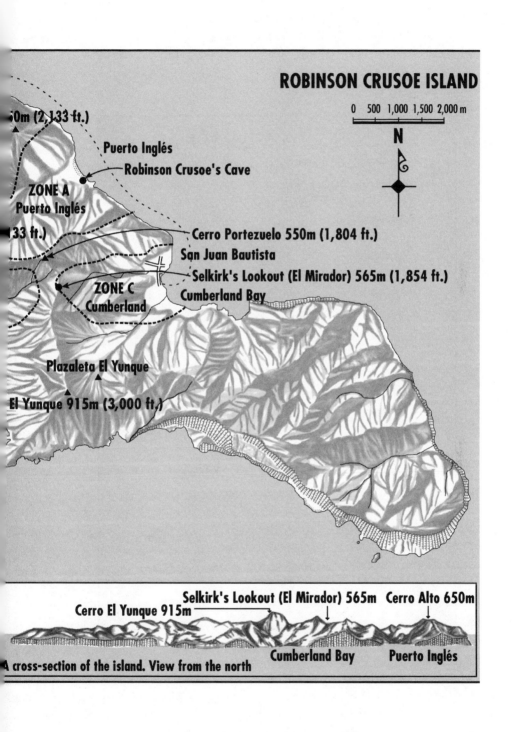

ROBINSON CRUSOE ISLAND

0   500 1,000 1,500 2,000 m

N

...0m (2,133 ft.)

Puerto Inglés

Robinson Crusoe's Cave

ZONE A
Puerto Inglés

...33 ft.)

Cerro Portezuelo 550m (1,804 ft.)

San Juan Bautista

Selkirk's Lookout (El Mirador) 565m (1,854 ft.)

ZONE C
Cumberland

Cumberland Bay

Plazaleta El Yunque

El Yunque 915m (3,000 ft.)

Cerro El Yunque 915m

Selkirk's Lookout (El Mirador) 565m   Cerro Alto 650m

Cumberland Bay   Puerto Inglés

A cross-section of the island. View from the north

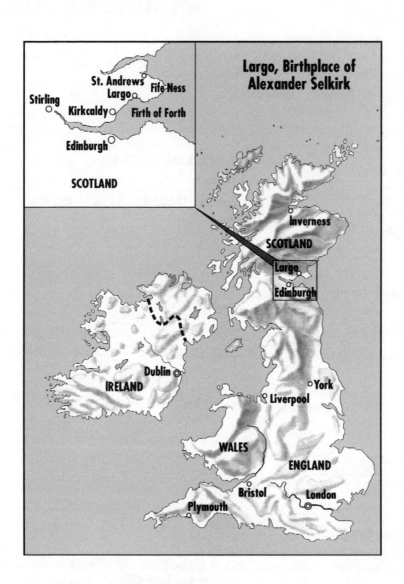

Largo, Birthplace of Alexander Selkirk

St. Andrews
Largo   Fife Ness
Stirling
Kirkcaldy   Firth of Forth
Edinburgh
SCOTLAND

Inverness
SCOTLAND
Largo
Edinburgh

IRELAND
Dublin

York
Liverpool

WALES

ENGLAND

Bristol
Plymouth   London

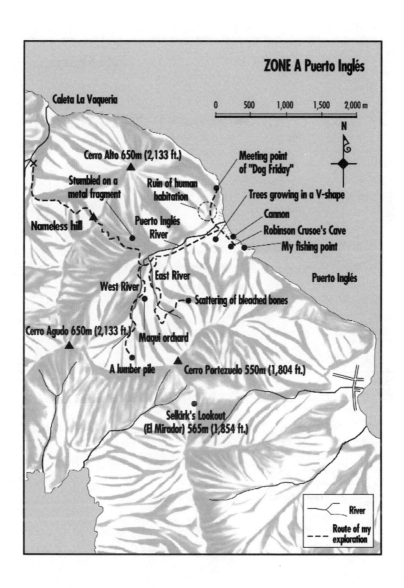

ZONE A Puerto Inglés

Caleta La Vaqueria

0   500   1,000   1,500   2,000 m

N

Cerro Alto 650m (2,133 ft.)

Meeting point of "Dog Friday"

Stumbled on a metal fragment

Ruin of human habitation

Trees growing in a V-shape

Cannon

Robinson Crusoe's Cave

Nameless hill

Puerto Inglés River

My fishing point

East River

West River

Puerto Inglés

Scattering of bleached bones

Cerro Agudo 650m (2,133 ft.)

Maqui orchard

A lumber pile

Cerro Portezuelo 550m (1,804 ft.)

Selkirk's Lookout (El Mirador) 565m (1,854 ft.)

River

Route of my exploration

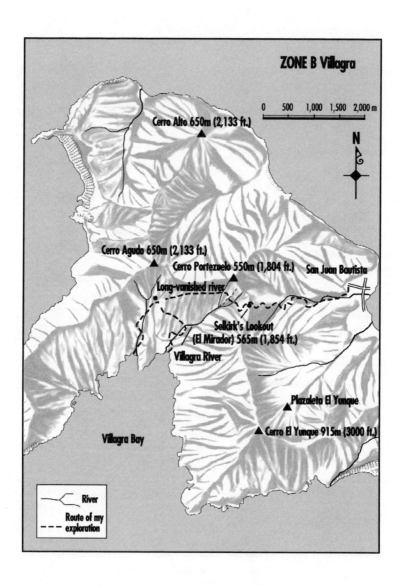

ZONE B Villagra

0   500   1,000   1,500   2,000 m

N

Cerro Alto 650m (2,133 ft.)

Cerro Agudo 650m (2,133 ft.)

Cerro Portezuelo 550m (1,804 ft.)

San Juan Bautista

Long-vanished river

Selkirk's Lookout
(El Mirador) 565m (1,854 ft.)

Villagra River

Plazaleta El Yunque

Cerro El Yunque 915m (3000 ft.)

Villagra Bay

River

Route of my
exploration

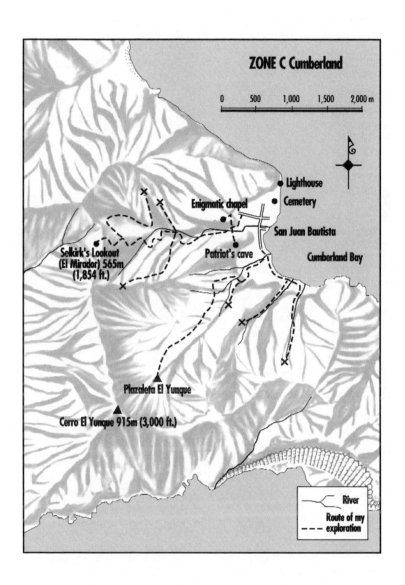

IN SEARCH OF

Robinson Crusoe

CHAPTER

One

On the Trail of a Three-Hundred-Year-Old Miracle

It was February 1994 in Oslo, Norway. As night drew in, the wind picked up, whirling icy snow through the streets. From the comfort of a warm bus I stared out at the frozen scene. Black tree silhouettes showed dimly through the falling snow, and lights from streetlights and houses flickered. The bus pulled cautiously out onto a main avenue, went past an old church, then rolled up before an imposing stone building. As the doors opened, a blast of cold air swept in all the way to the back of the bus. Everyone turned up their coat collars and got off the bus, moving through an ancient-looking gate and on indoors.

The building interior was pleasantly warm, and a big antique chandelier gave off a cheery blaze of light. One by one, we deposited our coats in the cloakroom and mounted carpeted stairs to the second floor, where waiters in formal dress were busily passing out welcome drinks. Champagne glasses in hand, we proceeded to mingle and chat with the 150 or so other guests in attendance, in front of a fireplace.

On hand were distinguished members of the Explorers Club, an organization with its headquarters in New York City. All sorts of adventurers were present, from every corner of the globe: men who had conquered Everest, marine explorers, jungle-dwelling biologists, archaeologists who patiently dug up desert sands, astronauts, designers of a future space station. This international conference in Oslo was meant to foster friendship and facilitate the exchange of information among explorers worldwide. Tonight's opening event was a formal dinner at the historic Norway Academy of Science, featuring Thor Heyerdahl as guest of honor.

There was a champagne toast, and then Heyerdahl spoke briefly. He was a hero and role model to everyone in the room. Half a century ago, his successful transoceanic voyage on the balsa raft *Kon-Tiki* enabled him to back his own daring theory that Pacific islanders are descended from ancient inhabitants of South America. In 1947, he built a primitive raft and set out from the coast of Peru, traveling the 7,000 kilometers [4,350 miles] to Tahiti at the mercy of ocean currents in an inspirational display of raw courage and devotion to truth.

Recalling the start of that voyage, Dr. Heyerdahl told us, "The main thing is to have faith in your convictions and your potential. That is what will always open up exploration of the unknown." I listened intently.

Finally the dinner ended, and with it the formal part of the evening. Now people got up and began again to talk to each other about their own adventures. The hall was filled to bursting with topics from every region on earth; with tales of every sort of undertaking, some successful, more not; with accounts of dreams, passions, ambitions. I, too, was drawn into absorbing conversation. I began to talk to the explorers about my own dreams and plans. Their curious eyes turned to me, full of interest.

The story of my own exploration began nearly three hundred years ago.

On February 2, 1709, Alexander Selkirk was rescued by a pair of English privateer vessels on the island of Mas-a-Tierra, far off the coast of Chile, bringing four years and four months of total isolation to an end. Two years and eight months later, on October 14, 1711, his long homeward voyage finally ended as well, as the ships docked safely in London, bringing him back to the homeland he had dreamed of for so long.

Once back, the Scot was hailed for his miraculous feat of survival in a far corner of the earth. But a few years afterwards, the men of the *Duke* and the *Duchess* would be even more surprised, as the man they found and rescued was fashioned into one of the greatest heroes of all time. On April 25, 1719, eight years after Selkirk's repatriation, Daniel Defoe published his immortal novel *The Life and Strange Surprising Adventures of Robinson Crusoe*, based on Selkirk's story. The bedraggled man the sailors picked up and brought home was the model for what eventually became one of the most famous characters in world fiction.

It was a most peculiar sight. February 1, 1709, in the South Pacific on the night when the uninhabited island they were aiming for, latitude 33°37' S, longitude 78°46' W, came into view, the 220-odd men on the English privateer vessels *Duke* and *Duchess* discovered a tiny light swaying on the otherwise dark island. No one could possibly be living there, and yet the presence of a reddish light was indisputable—a light that shone steadily bigger and brighter, the closer they came.

Could there be someone on the island?

The sailors left their stations and gathered on deck, entranced by the eerie sight. It was late at night, and a thin fog hung over the water. The mysterious light flickered with every gust of wind, swelling as the dark silhouette of the island loomed larger. Possessed by curiosity and dread, the men could only stand and watch, transfixed.

Captain Woodes Rogers, commander of the *Duke* and *Duchess*, shared his crew's uneasiness. That afternoon he had dispatched an exploratory team in a pinnace with Captain Dover at the helm, but no sign had been seen of them since sundown. When he first spotted the light, Captain Rogers had assumed it belonged to the pinnace; earlier, they had lit a lantern to keep the mother ship informed of their position, and had also fired shots from their quarter deck. Yet now something was different. The light from the island was getting bigger without any correlation to the signal from the boat. Clearly, it had some other source.

When the wind blew, flames stirred the darkness, staining it an eerie red. As commanding officer, what ought he to do under these circumstances? Captain Rogers was stumped.

His mind buzzed with possibilities. The likeliest explanation was a bonfire. Judging by its sheer size, there could be a huge number of people on the island. Or the enemy might be few in number, the large fire a ploy to scare off oncoming ships.

Either way, something nagged at him. They were close to shore now, with still no sign of any other ships to indicate a prior human presence. Then could the fire have been sparked by natural causes? No, he told himself, not on such a chilly night. What other logical explanation could there be? The sailors had begun muttering about "goblins" and "apparitions," but such talk only harked back to the days before anyone had ventured out onto the open seas, when fearful imaginations ran wild. Captain Rogers was a level-headed man, not one to be taken in by unfounded superstition. Yet the more rational he tried to be, the more trapped he was in a cul-de-sac of paradoxes, able only to stare at the light in bewilderment.

Around two in the morning, Captain Dover and his men returned, all safe, though exhausted after more than twelve hours of rowing. They had come within a stone's throw of shore, they reported, when the sun went down and the flames of a bonfire appeared on the edge of the island. There had been no sign of any boats, but the evidence of an enemy stronghold was persuasive enough for them to beat a swift retreat.

This account only deepened the mystery.

Next morning the sea was calm, the wind still. Gray clouds on the horizon lifted and the sun came out, lighting up the scene clearly. The island was enclosed in a vertical rock wall. Foamy waves hurled themselves again and again at the cliffs, bursting on impact. Rocky mountains towered, formed long ago by cooling torrents of lava, and in the distance glimpses of a deciduous forest could be seen.

A vast flock of stormy petrels flew by overhead, plummeting to the sea en masse the moment they spotted the dark shadow of a school of fish below the peaceful surface of the ocean. To the sailors, the birds' white plumage looked like scraps of paper dancing in the breeze. Then, amid the birds' clamoring, out of nowhere seals popped up, poking their innocent faces out of the water and looking the humans straight in the eye.

As dawn broke, Captain Rogers made his decision: he ordered the ships to swing round and sail for the island's shoreline. After contemplating the riddle all night long, he had decided the light belonged to treasure ships, and had come up with a plan to plunder them. During the night, wind and currents had driven the *Duke* and *Duchess* south. Now, catching a southerly wind, they headed for the opposite, northward, side. There was one bay on the island where large ships could weigh anchor, a natural harbor where several ships were bound to be moored— French, no doubt, laden high with priceless booty and cargo from South America. Captain Rogers was confident, remembering that in the Canary Islands off the northwest coast of Africa he had heard talk of five French vessels on their way to the South Seas.

His eagerness was only natural: he was the head of an authorized band of buccaneers who had left England and sailed all the way to the Pacific to get rich by attacking nearby treasure ships and stealing their precious cargoes.

Buccaneers though they were, a roving band of fierce pirates, the passage south from Europe through the wide oceans off the coast of South America, then north through the Pacific Ocean, had been excruciatingly long and painful. They'd left King Road in Bristol on August 2, 1708, rounding Cape Horn at the southernmost tip of South America five months later, on January 15, 1709, and moving thence to the waters of the Pacific. By January 25, after a period of rough seas amid constant cold gales and rain, the *Duchess* informed the *Duke* that her men were sick, and "want a Harbour to refresh 'em." To procure the necessary rest, water, and provisions, the ships had made for the island of Juan Fernandez, well known to seamen as one of the few in that part of the world to boast pure water and a plentiful supply of goats.

On January 31, 1709, the island came into view at seven in the morning, at a distance of seven leagues to the west-southwest. The light on shore had appeared the following day, arousing general amazement and dismay. Pirates they might be, but after their grueling voyage the men were in no condition to engage a rested enemy. Yet there was little choice. As Captain Rogers summed up in his log [*A Cruising Voyage round the World*], "we must either fight 'em or want Water." Battle preparations got underway.

As the ships drew near the eastern side of the island, Captain Rogers gave orders to proceed on around to the west, coming to anchor just before a promontory guarding the bay. Then he directed the crew of both ships to point their cannons toward the island, and assume firing positions. The order went out: "All hands, prepare for attack!"

Instantly, the ships were thrown into an uproar, the crews boiling with excitement. The long, difficult voyage was all a prelude to this moment. They would launch an attack, seize cargo and booty, and get rich—rich enough for a man to drink all the wine he could hold or take over an entire whorehouse. Some dreamed of the luxurious, profligate life they would lead back in England when it was all over, others of happily marrying the girl left behind.

When all arrangements were complete, the ships glided slowly over the water, crossing by the promontory until they could peer into the harbor. This was it, the moment of truth.

Not a single ship met their eyes, nor was there any sign of a human presence. Sea and shore alike were peaceful and deserted. Nonplussed, Captain Rogers ordered eight of his most trustworthy men ashore in the small pinnace, fully armed for a second reconnaissance expedition.

What was going on? The absence of any ship in the harbor could only mean there was nobody on shore, either—unless someone had moved to the island on a whim, which was hardly likely in such a godforsaken place. One could only conclude that last night's peculiar light had been an illusion or an apparition, the work of the devil.

After the pinnace was lowered and on its way, the sailors left behind maintained an uneasy silence, the squeaking of the mast the only sound on the gently swaying ships. One man up in the crow's nest kept a lookout with bated breath, but there was no sign of the reconnaissance squad.

An hour went by, then two. A pall hung over the two ships. Voices began to murmur that the light was the work of some evil spirit, after all. Captain Rogers pointed one of the cannons on the deck skyward and fired a blank as a signal for the boat to return. The ear-splitting noise echoed off the steep mountains, sending back a low sound like subterranean rumblings. When no response was forthcoming, Captain Rogers immediately sent out another pinnace full of armed men to investigate.

After a while, the cannon was fired again.

No answer from either boat.

The mysterious light of the night before, the empty harbor, the reconnaissance squads that had disappeared without a trace, the peaceful and silent sky, sea, island—none of it made any sense to Captain Rogers.

What should he do next?

In all his years on the sea, nothing so puzzling had ever happened before. As captain of a buccaneer ship, he was used to being the one on the attack, but now he found himself falling the apparent victim to the stratagems of some unknown entity.

Just then, the man in the crow's nest raised a loud cry: "They're headed back this way!"

"Both of 'em?"

"Yes!"

"Who's on board?"

The eagle-eyed sailor squinted hard.

For a while the men on deck remained quiet, praying hard that their shipmates had not been taken captive. The presence of a stranger on board the small craft would be a sign of the worst. As pirates, they had an instinct for trouble; besides, it was a trick they themselves often used.

The sailor aloft began to call out the names of the men in the order he recognized them. "Captain Dover . . . Mr. Frye . . ." When he had said the names of every man, he realized that in the back of the pinnace to the rear was one shadowy presence he could not for the life of him identify.

"And one more man . . ."

"A man? Who?"

A beam of slanting sunlight struck the boat for a moment, seeming to reveal a figure covered in fur.

"No, it's an animal . . ."

As the boat bounced up and down in the choppy waters, the dark figure moved in and out of sight.

"An animal, you say?"

"Yes, but . . . it looks human too . . ."

With the lives of everyone on board at stake, there was no room for error. The lookout opened his eyes wide, gazing more intently than ever, but not until the pinnace drew quite close did the nature of that dark figure become clear.

As the two boats pulled up to the ship, the sailors gasped in amazement at the totally unexpected sight. Speechless, they could not so much as cry out in surprise.

The dark shadow in the rear of the pinnace was revealed before their eyes as some sort of a wild man. His whiskers and beard were long and unkempt, and the skin of his face and hands was so deeply sunburned that his race was not immediately apparent. He wore a goatskin hat, a shirt, and trousers to the knee. Whether from excitement or from rage at being taken forcibly it was impossible to fathom, but tears streamed from his eyes.

Hoisted aboard the *Duke*, he began to sob again, and when spoken to, muttered incoherently. Seeing his evident distress at being unable to express himself, someone handed him tobacco and rum. He accepted the gifts joyfully, but the stimulation must have been too great, for the tobacco set him coughing, and no sooner did he take a swig of rum than he spat it all out.

As soon as they landed on shore, said the scouts, a hairy man had come running up to them with remarkable force. Fearing he was a monster or savage, they felt a chill of terror; it was all they could do to draw their knives to protect themselves, and their legs shook.

Then something totally unexpected happened. As the savage drew near, he spoke words they knew well: "Help me, I . . . I . . . I . . ." At any rate, he apparently meant them no harm. The eight men gathered round him on the shore and listened intently, trying to make out who he was and what he was attempting to convey.

It soon was clear from the man's halting speech that he had not used language for a long time. The sounds emerging from his mouth were English, but he seemed to speak by halves, as it were, so it was all they could do to make sense of what he said. Some were of the opinion that he was from an enemy country, a foreigner who knew only a smattering of English. When they finally pieced together his story, it went something like this:

He was from Scotland, and his name was Alexander Selkirk. The day before, on seeing British ships approach, he had frantically lit a signal fire, forgoing food and rest to keep it stoked night and day. He was the lone inhabitant of the island. Some untoward series of events had conspired to deposit him there, but how long he had been there, they could not make out.

He led them inland to a pair of huts he himself had built. Confronted by the reality of the life he had carved out single-handedly, they felt profound shock.

For the next ten days, the *Duke* and the *Duchess* stayed anchored at the island, to rest and gather water and provisions.

This Morning we clear'd up Ship, and bent our Sails, and got them ashore to mend, and make Tents for our sick Men. The

*Governour (tho we might as well have nam'd him the Absolute
Monarch of the Island) for so we call'd Mr. Selkirk, caught us
two Goats, which make excellent Broth, mix'd with Turnip-Tops
and other Greens, for our sick Men, being 21 in all, but not
above two that we account dangerous; the* Duchess *has more
Men sick, and in a worse condition than ours. . . .*

*. . . A few Men supply us all with Fish of several sorts, all very
good; as Silver-fish, Rock-fish, Pollock, Cavallos, Oldwives, and
Craw-fish in such abundance, that in a few hours we could take
as many as would serve some hundreds of Men. There were Sea-
Fowls in the Bay as large as Geese, but eat fish. The Governour
never fail'd of getting us two or three Goats a day for our sick
Men, by which with the help of the Greens and the Goodness of
the Air they recover'd very fast of the Scurvy, which was their general Distemper.*[1]

The man knew all there was to know about the island,
as well he might after having lived there so long in total
isolation. Edible plants including turnips, watercress, cabbage trees, parsley, and purslain; pimento wood, which
made excellent firewood; coves of good water—his knowledge of all these and more was a great boon to the weary
sailors in need of replenishing their stores. Moreover, he
himself would dive into the sea and swim about like a fish,
seizing large crayfish from under rocks, or dash off barefoot, scampering with amazing speed through the hills,
and come back with a live goat on his back.

Everything he did, whether it was swimming, or running up and down mountains, or fishing and hunting
without rod or gun, made the men doubt their own
eyes. Not even the bulldog they had brought along was

---

1. Woodes Rogers, *A Cruising Voyage round the World* (London: Bell
and B. Lintot, 1712), pp. 123–37.

able to keep pace with him, coming back winded and exhausted.

In the days immediately following his rescue, the man gradually recovered his composure, but his speech was still a muddle. It took awhile before he was able to give them a lucid account of the terrible fate that had befallen him and of the life he had created on that uninhabited island. Of all the tales they had ever heard at sea, his was the most deeply impressive and solemn of all. He too had been a buccaneer, which made them listen all the more intently. It could have happened to any of them.

The true adventures of Alexander Selkirk, the man whose story provided such inspiration for Defoe, have today all but passed from public memory. I myself stumbled onto his story by chance as I was translating a history of world explorations published by the Royal Geographical Society, where I read a spare, 350-word account.

Nowadays exploration is often taken to mean the probing of unknown realms in ever-more specialized fields of science, leaving amateurs like myself to sit idly on the sidelines. Yet in the course of my translation of the society's *History of World Exploration,* I came across one small column that I sensed could change my life. It told of a man left behind for a trifling reason on an uninhabited island in the South Seas.

I learned that about three hundred years ago, Alexander Selkirk, an eighteenth-century sailor of Scotch origin, had a difference of opinion with the captain of the privateer vessel he was on and unluckily wound up spending four years and four months on a tiny deserted island far off the coast of Chile. I also learned that he was the talk of London following his return, inspiring Daniel Defoe to write *Robinson Crusoe* based on Selkirk's experience, the details of which Defoe adapted as he pleased—including increasing the length of the exile.

Having assumed all my life that Robinson Crusoe was a fictional character, I reacted to this news with shock. Had it been an ordinary shipwreck story, my interest would not have been aroused. But to think, a real Robinson Crusoe! The short account gripped me setting my imagination on fire.

Born in 1966 in the northern Japanese prefecture of Akita, surrounded by lush nature, I had read *Robinson Crusoe* as a boy and felt vaguely drawn to the world it portrayed. I would catch fish in a nearby stream and grill them over a fire, or plant sticks in the family backyard, absorbed in the puzzle of how to build myself a hut. To my parents, I must have seemed a typically mischievous kid, but in my own eyes, those were serious endeavors. What if I were stranded on a deserted island like Crusoe? Would I be able to survive by constructing a shelter and learning to hunt the way he did? For me, as for countless readers of the book, Defoe's tale lit a flame in my mind, sparking a love for adventure that lasted into my adult years.

During college, I trekked across six of the earth's continents with a backpack holding my sleeping bag and supplies. "Nature and man" was the theme of my wanderings, as I tried to establish how well I could get on in the wild. My travels took me to the Amazon River and the Sahara Desert, to the Himalayas and Siberia, to Southeast Asia and dense tropical forests, to the arid Australian Outback, even as far as the Antarctic. In each of these inhospitable regions, I would sigh in despair, "I could never do it. I could never live here."

No matter how much I loved nature, a city-bred person like myself had no chance of adapting as easily to a harsh environment as the people born there. But what if someone handicapped by a lifetime spent in the daily comforts of modern civilization was thrown all of a sudden into nature, with no prior knowledge or preparation? How could he manage? Would someone like me really be able to survive? None of the people I had encountered on the fringes of civilization gave any answer to that simple question. They had all been born into a culture adapted to the environment.

What sparked my interest in that riddle lay inside the book that had remained my bible everywhere I went: *Robinson Crusoe*. And now I knew that it was not a mere work of fiction after all.

What were the adventures and the life of the real Robinson Crusoe, Alexander Selkirk, like? He set off as a sailor in the eighteenth century, just before the Industrial Revolution worked its vast changes on society, leaving civilization behind and ending up a lone castaway on a solitary island in the distant sea, with no special tools or knowledge to aid in his survival. What had he eaten, how had he lived? What worries beset him, what discoveries did he make, how did he go about building a life? Here lay the real story of human ingenuity in the wilderness, its potential and its limitations.

I decided to excavate Selkirk's life: the circumstances he fell into, the decisions he made and actions he took, the hopes and dreams he nursed, the frustration and despair he was prey to. All of these I would exhume from the ashes of history. I would also have to try to relive a little of his experience myself. In order to give me a taste of his life on the deserted island, I would have to go there, taking with me only the tools and food essential for survival. I would also get to fulfill my boyhood dream.

CHAPTER

Two

Selkirk's Early Days

My journey to unravel the life and adventures of Alexander Selkirk began in a fog.

In the late spring of 1993, I combed libraries and did the rounds of the used-book stores in Kanda, Tokyo, uncovering reams of material. All my efforts were wasted, however, as no new clues came to light. The existence of a real-life prototype of Robinson Crusoe seemed to be common knowledge, especially among literary scholars and Defoe specialists, but the specialists' sole concern was interpreting the novel. No one had done any research on Selkirk, let alone paid a visit to the island where he was marooned.

I reread the novel again and again, searching for any sort of clue. Question after question presented itself. How much of the novel was fiction, how much fact? Was the novel's other main character, Friday, totally imaginary?

For the sake of readers who may not yet have read *Robinson Crusoe,* or who may have forgotten it, here is a brief sketch of the plot.

Robinson Kreutzner (his name is later anglicized to Crusoe), the adventure-loving son of a merchant, ignores his father's advice to take over the family business and instead becomes a sailor. During the course of one voyage, his ship runs into a storm and runs aground. Robinson washes up half-dead and alone on the shore of a small, solitary island. At first he is lonely and terrified, but eventually, recognizing his good fortune in being the lone survivor, he becomes convinced that he will one day be rescued. He devotes himself to a life of prayer and Bible reading, enduring twenty-eight years, two months, and nineteen days of solitary existence.

During that time, Crusoe contrives with indomitable patience and creativity to build a life for himself. Using materials from the wrecked ship, he constructs a house and fills it with furniture, plants wheat and bakes bread, goes hunting and captures goats. Out of goatskin, he fashions shirts, trousers, and an umbrella. As companions, a dog, a cat, and a parrot he names Poll provide temporary diversion; later, an aborigine from a neighboring island comes over and becomes his servant. He names him "Friday," after the day of the week on which Crusoe saved him from being eaten alive by his own cannibalistic tribe.

One day, an English pirate ship drops anchor at sea by the island. A mutiny has taken place aboard the ship, and the captain and two other men are being held captive. With Friday's help, Crusoe cleverly punishes the miscreants and takes control of the ship. Thus, at long last the way is opened for him to return home, and he is repatriated to England.

A castaway on a deserted island overcoming loneliness and fear to carve out an active and forward-looking life— in this story of one man's checkered fate, and his response to it, is a timeless account of what it means to be human.

Having discovered the lack of material available in Japan, I wrote for help to the Royal Geographical Society in London, the Explorers Club in New York, and a used-book dealer in San Diego whom I had known for some seven years. After spotting an ad in the transactions of the Explorers Club declaring his specialty to be "books on mountain climbing and exploration," I had gotten in the habit of writing to him for assistance whenever anything came up. Over the years, although we have never met, he has always managed to come up with a satisfying answer to whatever knotty problem I toss his way.

And yet, at first my attempts were in vain.

Even so, everyone whom I contacted was kind enough to introduce me to every person and institution they could think of, and through exchanges of letters, I was eventually able to obtain copies of various magazine articles published in the United Kingdom and the United States. Most were not directly connected with my theme,

but a glance at the bibliographies revealed the existence
of five sources treating either Selkirk's adventures or the
story of his life:

A Cruising Voyage round the World, *by Captain Woodes
Rogers, 1712*
A Voyage to the South Seas and round the World, *by Captain
Edward Cooke, 1712*
The Life and Adventures of Alexander Selkirk, *by John
Howell, 1829*
The Real Robinson Crusoe, *by R.L. Mégroz, 1939*
An essay by Richard Steel in The Englishman, *December 3, 1713*

Of these, the first three are firsthand accounts by personal acquaintances of Selkirk; the fourth, a magnum
opus based on interviews with relatives and descendants
of his in possession of various documents; and the last,
a compendium of the first four. Together, they contained all the background material I would need for my
research and exploration, and for the writing of this
book.

Yet since their publication many years had passed.
They were all out of print, and there was no guarantee
that I would ever get my hands on any of them. My
friend the book dealer wrote, "If you don't mind waiting
a few years, I'll do all I can." For a while I heard no
more. Almost two years had gone by when he sent word
that he had got hold of some of the books. After two
more years, I was able to obtain all five, as well as a
wealth of other books and materials.

Then began a tough regimen of getting up at dawn
every workday, and spending every holiday glued to my
desk from morning to night, poring over those tattered
old texts with constant reference to a dictionary. I kept

notes as I read, and I went over them again and again, pondering.

Almost every account of Alexander Selkirk's life on the deserted island was based on *A Cruising Voyage round the World* by Captain Woodes Rogers, the sea captain who rescued Selkirk and took him home to England. The account centers on his discovery and rescue of Selkirk, with some description of Selkirk's life on the island, but, unfortunately, it is mostly a record of the captain's astonishment, with little attention to the details of Selkirk's feat. Of course, the captain had no way of knowing that the castaway he rescued would ever become so famous.

After that, a number of books and articles appeared at regular intervals over the years, but none of them went beyond quotations or extracts from Captain Rogers's account. I was still largely in the dark, not only about Selkirk's life on the island but also about his origins, his boyhood, and his life before becoming a sailor.

I did come across one important piece of information, however: in the country village of Largo, in Scotland, the house where he was born still existed, and it contained a statue of him. What was his family background, what sort of youth had he experienced? My only hope of finding out was to go there myself.

On February 5, 1994, en route to Norway to attend that international convention of the Explorers Club, I flew from Japan to London, then up to Edinburgh.

Largo, the village of Selkirk's birth, in the County of Fife, is across the Firth of Forth from Edinburgh and so small that only a very detailed map will include it. The surrounding land is extremely hilly. At the end of a road leading out of the village to the northeast is St. Andrews, the renowned birthplace of golf, and indeed the map I used was dotted with golf courses. Little rivers penetrate deeply inland like capillaries, pouring into ponds and lochs and winding through coniferous forests before leading again to the sea.

Largo is built directly on the Firth of Forth, and its shoreline consists of approximately two and a half kilometers of beach where people from nearby no doubt gather in summer. I, however, was going there in midwinter. I imagined it would be a quiet, rather lonely place.

The middle-aged woman at the information counter in the airport didn't even seem sure where Largo was. When I showed her my map, she at last got her bearings. "You want to take the airport bus to Edinburgh Station, then get on the train for Kirkcaldy, and take the bus from there," she advised me.

It sounded dubious to me. Night was coming on; would I truly be able to find my way there, having no feel for the area? Besides, there was no telling what accommodations I might find in Largo, if any. I'd have to prepare myself for a night on a bench in the train or bus station, if need be. In spite of my misgivings, I boarded the airport bus for Edinburgh's Waverley railway station, hoping for the best.

Getting off at Kirkcaldy was like slipping back in time to the Middle Ages. The surroundings appeared ancient, and although the hour was just past 9:30 P.M., the entire town was fast asleep. There was no one around for me to ask where the bus terminal was, and I couldn't believe that buses would be running in that deep, foggy darkness anyway.

I was stranded alone in the dead of winter, with no idea where to go. The vague apprehension I had been feeling all along was now justified. What to do? Should I stroll around, or go back to the station and look for a bench to spend the night on?

But as I was wandering around disconsolately, what should come along but an empty taxicab. Quickly I raised my arm and hailed it. "I want to go to Largo."

The surroundings were dark and deserted, this was a back street in a country town far from any tourist attractions, and I was an Asian man with a day's growth of beard—small wonder that the cabby was wary at first. But as I explained the reason for my trip, he brightened and gestured for me to sit in the passenger seat, declaring that he knew just the place.

After a twenty-minute ride through dark, rolling country, the taxi entered a tiny village and stopped in front of a hotel facing the water. The sign read "The Crusoe Hotel." The cabby told me, "Robinson Crusoe's old house is near here, and there's a statue of him, too. Oh, and a descendant of the real fellow lives nearby, too, so you should go see him tomorrow. He'll tell you all you need to know." And with that he drove back the way he came.

The Crusoe Hotel was a very quiet, snug little place. I stepped up to the reception desk and said tentatively, "I came here to meet with the descendant of the real Robinson Crusoe." The girl didn't bat an eyelash. "He was over there, drinking at the bar until a wee while ago."

Next to the front desk was indeed a dim bar marked "The Juan Fernandez Bar." Behind the polished counter were neat rows of unfamiliar-looking bottles of Scotch whisky.

I could barely repress my excitement: having stumbled on this place purely by chance, I now had the priceless opportunity for an encounter with Selkirk's descendant. Still, it tickled me to think of a descendant of the real-life Robinson Crusoe coming in for a drink at the Crusoe Hotel, of all places!

The room I was shown to was decked out like a ship's cabin and proved most comfortable. The window looked straight out on the firth, and I could hear the roar of waves close by. When I opened the window, a fresh sea breeze swept into the room. The firth was big and wild. This was what Selkirk had grown up seeing, what had inspired him to become a sailor.

When I awoke at 7:30 all was still dark outside, with just a tinge of brightness in the eastern sky. After watching the extremely late sunrise that February morning, I stepped outside to take a walking tour of the chilly village.

I found Largo to be a tranquil village with a population of barely fifteen hundred. Situated on the slope of a gentle hill, it is divided into two parts: Upper Largo at the top of the hill, and Lower Largo at the bottom, close to the water's edge. Along the waterfront stood solidly built stone houses; the top of the hill was forested, with pastureland spreading below. Though my breath showed white in the frosty air, the meadows were covered with bright green grass that never turned brown in winter. A dozen sheep were milling around; when they noticed me, they stood stock still and gave me steady looks.

In the late seventeenth century, when Selkirk lived here, the place flourished as a center of the fishing industry, supported by bountiful catches from the North Sea. In time, however, the fishing fell off for whatever reason, and so did the population. Now carpenters and laborers manage to eke out a living, but only a handful of fishermen are to be found, and most of the residents are elderly. At day's end, men of working age gather in the hotel bar for a drink, but their places of work are elsewhere, in Kircaldy or Edinburgh.

Summers in Largo are delightful but short; the long autumn has a dispiriting effect on people. An Arctic front extends over the area, causing a low pressure area to settle in so that a solid bank of gray clouds hangs heavily overhead, covering up the sky.

After breakfast, I mentioned to the manager my interest in meeting the descendant of "Robinson Crusoe," and he kindly arranged a get-together with a man called Allan Jardine.

The young man who showed up at the hotel struck me as a rough and ruggedly honest type. He was wearing a marine-style blazer covered with gold buttons, his hair was long, and he sported a scraggly beard. "What'll you have?" he asked.

He seated himself on the sofa and ordered a pint of lager. "You took me by surprise. I never thought anyone would travel halfway around the world just to see me," he said, and carefully held out a book to show me. "My mother was something of an amateur historian, and she wrote this history of Largo. Alexander Selkirk is in here, too."

I started out by asking him his connection to Selkirk, the legendary figure of three hundred years ago.

"He was the younger brother of my great-grandfather's great-grandfather's grandfather."

As I was silent, stumped for a reply, Jardine flipped through the pages of the history that his mother had published at her own expense, titled *Seatoun*[sic] *of Largo*, and thrust it at me. It was opened to a Selkirk family tree. Alexander, it turned out, was the seventh child born to John Selcraig and Eufan Mackie, who wed in 1657. Jardine was the direct descendant of their firstborn, David. The family tree continued without a break from 1657, showing eight generations from Alexander Selkirk to Allan Jardine.

I made up my mind to read all the history I could find, beginning with Jardine's *Seatoun of Largo* and including the accounts of Selkirk's origins and youth in the books by Howell and Mégroz.

Alexander Selkirk, destined to become the real-life model for the fictional character of Robinson Crusoe, was born in 1676, the twentieth year of his parents' marriage. His father, John Selcraig, made a good living as a tanner and cobbler. A Presbyterian, he was a man of clean habits and integrity whose prosperity no doubt owed in large part to his stern moral uprightness. Alexander's mother, Eufan, was quite another story, a romantic whose influence, it is said, led nearly all of her seven boys to elect the life of the sea. Only Alexander strayed far from home, however, the rest becoming fishermen in nearby waters.

When he was old enough to attend the Kirk school in Largo, Alexander's natural liveliness came to the fore, causing him to band together with neighborhood boys and go around getting into all sorts of mischief. As he grew older, he, like his brothers before him, was drawn to the sea, and he did well at school in subjects like mathematics and geography.

Most of the village fishermen fished only a few miles off the coast, but a few ventured out onto the open sea. To young Alexander, bored with the even tenor of life in Largo, the stories they brought back were fresh and exciting, the very essence of adventure. There were stories of a near-escape from cannibals in African jungles; of shooting down a charging lion in savanna; of finding hidden treasure on a deserted island. Enthralled, Alexander vowed that as soon as he was old enough, he too would become a sailor and travel around the world.

He talked over his future with his parents a number of times, always insisting he would be a sailor and nothing else, but his stern and conservative father would hear nothing of it, categorically refusing to consider his son's wishes. As far as John Selcraig was concerned, the only men who should became sailors were those who knew no trade or missionaries with a noble intent to spread truth to benighted lands. For anyone else, it amounted to throwing your life away. Honest work was the shortest route to happiness, he counseled his young son, and the pathway to God. He urged Alexander to follow in his own footsteps and take over the family business of tanning when he finished school.

At the same time, his mother Eufan secretly supported his dream. To her, life ought to be dramatic. A man ought to pit himself bravely against some stiff challenge and win the victory. Such feats were a mother's pride; children's successes could bring great change to a mother's life, too.

This tendency to romanticize the sea may have been especially prevalent among common people of the day. For a tanner and cobbler like John Selcraig, average annual income was some forty pounds. In contrast, a middle-class trading merchant might earn as much as two hundred pounds a year.

In his pamphlet, *A Plan of the English Commerce,* Defoe comments, "that tho' they say, the Tradesman cannot be made Gentlemen; yet the Tradesmen are, at this Time, able to buy the Gentlemen almost in every part of the Kingdom."[1]

And yet a hard-nosed realist would find the opposition of Selkirk's father persuasive. A sailor's annual wages were less than twenty pounds, and an apprentice with no seafaring experience or skills could expect to receive little or nothing. Being a sailor meant living far from one's family, with death an ever-present threat; compared to the life of an artisan, the risk was far too great.

Alexander Selkirk's infancy and childhood occurred in a transitional time of history, as thirty years of constant civil strife and war came to an end in Britain and a new age got underway. The Civil War of 1642–48 had culminated in the defeat and beheading of Charles I and the establishment of a new republican Commonwealth. That state of affairs was not to last long, however, for the monarchy was reestablished in 1660 with the accession of Charles II, thus reviving the Stuart dynasty.

Tears of grief for the many war victims were barely dried before the next disaster struck: in 1665, London was swept by the feared pestilence known as the Black Death. The hot months of August and September saw the plague reach its zenith, felling as many as 550,000 people in all, it is said, at an average of 1,000 per day. The very next year brought the Great Fire that nearly destroyed the city. On

---

1. Daniel Defoe, *A Plan of the English Commerce* (London: William Clowes & Sons, 1974), p. 61.

Sunday, September 2, 1666, fire broke out in a bakery on Pudding Lane near London Bridge in central London. A preceding spell of dry weather contributed to the quick spread of flames throughout the city. For four days the fire raged, consuming 12,300 homes and reducing the streets of London to ash.

Twenty years later, political events culminated in the Glorious Revolution, as a result of which the Dutch prince William of Orange became William III, joint sovereign with his consort Mary II, and a constitutional monarchy was born.

Despite all this turbulence, life was by no means entirely dismal. The first coffee house appeared in London in 1652; thirty years later, there were three thousand, as people grew accustomed to drinking coffee, tea, and chocolate on a daily basis. These new gathering places also proved to be great places for the exchange of information. A variety of periodical publications came out that would evolve later into daily newspapers, along with a dazzling assortment of new fashions from tobacco, canes, and umbrellas to male wigs.

In London and elsewhere, the trend of the times was moving away from the old-fashioned, church-dominated society of medieval times toward a modern, parliamentary society. But deep in the Scottish countryside in the village of Largo, the church still held sway, dominating administrative affairs. In the heart of Kirkton parish stood Largo Parish Church, dating from the fourteenth century, where the Session, consisting of the Presbyterian Elders and the minister, would meet to discuss such important matters as payment of school fees for children of the poor. In addition to being a holy place of worship, the church was also the hub of village life and the seat of village administration.

Alexander dreamed of becoming a sailor, yet his father stubbornly refused to allow it. The boy was full of pent-up frustration and anger. Finally, in 1695, when he was nineteen years old, he assaulted someone in church. Session minutes for 1695 contain the following verbatim account:

> *Alexander Selchraig to be summoned. August 25. This same day the Session mett. The qlk[2] day Alexr Selchraig, son of John Selchraig, elder, in Nether Largo, was dilated[3] for his undecent beaiver in ye church; the church officer is ordirred to go and cite him to compear[4] befoor our Session agst ye nixt dyett. August 27, ye Session mett. Alexander Selchraige did not compear. The qlk day Alexander Selchraig, son of John Selchraige, elder, in Nether Largo, called, but did not compear, being gone away to ye seas; this business is continued til his return.*

In an age when the church was of central importance in society, Alexander had committed a desecration against God, no doubt a more serious offense than we can easily imagine today. To his Presbyterian father, it was perhaps the ultimate act of filial impiety, worse even than becoming a sailor.

After this incident, Alexander disappears from the village for six years, vanishing without a trace, but then one day in 1701 he turns up again unexpectedly. He informs his parents and brothers that he has indeed become a sailor and traveled all over, but he shows no sign of compunction, nor does he seem concerned in the slightest

---

2. Short for *quhilk*, a form of the Anglo-Saxon *hwile* (which).
3. reported
4. appear

about his past misdeeds. In fact, probably because of the rough company he has been keeping aboard ship, he is more hot-headed, more prone to think with his fists, than ever before. No sooner is he back than he is again involved in a fracas, this time inflicting injury on his own brothers. Session minutes offer a fairly detailed account of the trouble.

November 1701. The same day, John Guthrie delated John Selcraig, elder, and his wife Euphan Mackie, and Alexander Selcraig, for disagreement together, and also John Selcraig, and his wife, Margaret Bell. All of them are ordered to be cited against the next session, which is to be the 25th instant.

November 25. The same day, John Selcraig, elder, being called, compeared, and being examined what was the occasion of the tumult that was in his house, he said he knew not; but that Andrew Selcraig having brought in a can full of salt water, of which his brother Alexander did take a drink through mistake, and he laughing at him for it, his brother Alexander came and beat him, upon which he ran out of the house and called his brother John.

John Selcraig, elder, being again questioned what made him to sit upon the floor with his back at the door, he said it was to keep down his son Alexander, who was seeking to go up to get down his pistol. And being inquired what he was going to do with it? he said he could not tell.

The same day, Alexander Selcraig called, appeared not. He was at Cupar. He is to be cited pro secundo against the next session.

The same day, John Selcraig, younger, called, appeared, and being questioned concerning the tumult that was in his father's house of the 7th November last, declared, that he being called by his brother Andrew, came to it, and when he entered the house his mother went out, and he, seeing his father sitting upon the floor with his brother at the door, was much troubled, and offered to help him up, and to bring him to the floor; at which time he did see his brother Alexander in the other end of the house, casting off his coat, and coming towards him, whereupon his father did get up, and coming towards him, did get betwixt them, but he knew not what he did otherways, his head being borne down by his brother Alexander; but afterwards being liberated by his wife, he made his escape.

Same day, Margaret Bell called, appeared, and being inquired what was the occasion of the tumult which fell out in her father-in-law's house on the seventh November, she said, that Andrew Selcraig came running for her husband John, and desiring him to go to his father's house; which he doing, the said Margaret did follow her husband, and, coming into the house, she found the said Alexander gripping both his father and her husband, and she labouring to loose his hands from her husband's head and breast, her husband fled out of doors, and she followed him, and called back again, 'You false loon, will you murder your father and my husband both?' whereupon he followed her to the door; but whether he beat her or not, she was in so great confusion, she cannot say distinctly, but ever since she hath a sore pain in her head.

The same day, Andrew Selcraig called, appeared, but said nothing to purpose in the aforesaid business. This business is delayed until the next session until farther inquiry be made.

November 29. Alexander Selcraig, scandalous for contention and disagreeing with his brothers, called, appeared, and being questioned concerning the tumult that was in his house, whereof he was said to be the occasion, he confessed that, he having taken a drink of salt water out of a can, his younger brother Andrew laughing at him for it, he did beat him twice with a staff. He confessed also that he had spoken very ill words concerning his brother, and particularly he challenged his elder brother, John, to a combat, as he called it, of dry neifs, ells then, he said, he would not care even to do it now, which afterwards he did refuse and regrate; moreover he said several things, whereupon the session *appointed him to appear before the face of the congregation for his scandalous carriage.*

November 30. Alexander Selcraig, according to the session's appointment, appeared before the pulpit, and made acknowledgment of his sin in disagreeing with his brothers, and was rebuked in the face of the congregation for it, and promised amendment in the strength of the Lord, and so was dismissed.

The villagers could no longer condone such behavior from the son of a pious Presbyterian. Alexander receives a formal reprimand in church and leaves Largo behind, moving on like a drifter. The village has forsaken him, and he likewise abandons his homeland. From that time on, he formally changes the spelling of his surname from Selcraig to the English "Selkirk."

Approximately two years later, on March 9, 1703, two armed merchant ships set sail from Kinsale, Ireland: the *St. George*, led by Captain William Dampier, and the galley *Cinque Ports*, led by Captain Charles Pickering. Together they formed a privateer band and headed for the Pacific Ocean, hoping to make their fortune in the South Sea.

Pirating—also known as privateering—expeditions such as this received formal commissions from the monarch of England to attack and plunder enemy ships, usually vessels of commerce. At the same time, they were an effective form of harassment against Spain, whose successful initiatives in the New World were of great annoyance to England. It was, in effect, officially sanctioned guerilla warfare.

Captain William Dampier was well known among seamen as a privateer, which is to say a big-shot pirate. His book *A New Voyage round the World*, published in 1679, was an immediate success and spread his renown among ordinary citizens as well. Later he failed in his command of a warship in the English navy, but his record as a privateer earned him a second chance, and so he set off on this voyage to the South Sea with nearly two hundred men under his command. Also on board was Alexander Selkirk, whose whereabouts for the previous two years remain unaccounted for.

Selkirk's determination to cross the seas and his devotion to sailing must have been extraordinary; he managed to acquire brilliant navigational skills in only a few years. By the time he signed up with the galley *Cinque Ports,* he had attained the important post of sailing-master; it was his job to determine the ship's location and ensure that it stayed on course. Every thirty minutes, he had to change the man at the helm and enter the ship's course and speed in the log.

The ships sailed southward from Ireland across the Atlantic Ocean toward the southern tip of South America, where they rounded Cape Horn and entered the Pacific Ocean. Both vessels were heavily overloaded with crew, and living and working conditions were filthy and inferior. Provision stores turned into hotbeds of rats and roaches, and as the voyage progressed, it became necessary to brush off worms and animal droppings before consuming so much as a single biscuit.

On a trip halfway around the world and back, under these terrible living conditions, the sailors became embroiled in one personal altercation after another. What started it all was the sudden death of Captain Charles Pickering aboard the *Cinque Ports.* After Pickering's death, his second in command, Lieutenant Thomas Stradling, assumed the post of captain, but his tyrannical arrogance soon got the men's backs up. Selkirk, ever the hothead, quarreled constantly with him. Stradling even had violent disagreements with Captain Dampier, chief commander of the expedition, and more than once the two vessels were on the verge of parting company.

In February 1704, they spotted a huge, four-hundred-ton French ship and commenced hostilities, only to suffer ignominious defeat. The *St. George* suffered nine fatalities and numerous wounded. After that, they came across two fully armed French ships, but avoided combat.

In March, they spotted a small Spanish ship. Again going on the attack, this time they managed to plunder it of coins, clothing, tobacco, tar, and indigo. They repeated their success with another small Spanish ship in April, and Dampier took aboard an Englishman who had been held captive on the enemy ship.

By now they had spent some six months in the Pacific. Their piratical successes were limited to small ships, and for all the distance they had come and the risks they had taken, they had very little to show. Worse, as the voyage lengthened, provisions began to run out. Full of impatience and indignation, the seamen began to grumble, and to take out their pent-up feelings on each other.

Then, off the coast of Peru they allowed a great 150-ton Spanish galleon to slip through their fingers. The hold of the merchant galleon was estimated to be full of enough linen and wool to command a fortune back in Europe, as well as flour, salt, sugar, brandy, wine, and thirty tons of marmalade besides. Someone claimed that eighty thousand dollars' worth of gold had been concealed in the bottom of the hold as well. The sailors' resentment ignited, and they began demanding that Captain Dampier take responsibility for the failure.

Shipboard conditions and morale remained bad, and in May, when they reached the latitude of Panama Bay, the two ships split up.

Once rid of Captain Dampier and the *St. George,* Stradling grew still more lordly and domineering. Selkirk, his sailing-master, being quick-tempered by nature, was unable to let anything slide, and undaunted by Stradling's high-handedness, he continued to rebel. As relations between the two men steadily deteriorated, the situation was ripe for explosion.

Some of the men sided with Selkirk, but no one was willing to go so far as to declare a mutiny and wrest control from the captain. Selkirk's violent tendencies made him unfit as a leader, and he did not enjoy enough popularity among the men to unite them behind him.

After pillaging its way across the seas off the coast of central South America, the *Cinque Ports* headed for the deserted island of Mas-a-Tierra in the Juan Fernandez Archipelago. The galley was leaking water and badly in need of repair. Supplies of fresh water, meat, and vegetables were low, as were supplies of lumber and firewood.

In September 1704, signs of spring were in the air; the breeze had a new mildness and fragrance, and the sailor's hearts were softened. When they dropped anchor at Mas-a-Tierra, they found new grass poking up through the ground and new leaves in bud on the trees. Water in the streams was warm to the touch, and large numbers of birds were pecking at tender shoots along the water's edge. But these days of ease and relaxation were not to last long.

Some small thing pitted Captain Stradling's haughtiness against Selkirk's temper, and Selkirk finally burst out,

"The hell with this ship. I'm damned if I ever sail with you again."

Nothing could have pleased Stradling more than for this irritant to disappear forever from his sight. Leaving Selkirk there on the deserted island would be the perfect warning to the rest of the crew, too. He deliberately spoke even more harshly, goading Selkirk into deserting ship.

The *Cinque Ports* remained moored at the island for three full days, replenishing its food and other supplies. When it was time to set sail again, Selkirk's meager belongings were toted ashore.

As he watched the men's hasty preparations to leave, Selkirk reflected on his behavior and reconsidered. The animosity he felt for Stradling was nothing compared to the loneliness and terror of being left utterly alone. Anxiety and sadness gripped him by the throat until finally he capitulated. He went to Stradling and apologized, stating clearly that he'd been wrong and begging to be let back on board. He swore he would not rebel anymore and would obey the captain's every command.

Captain Stradling listened attentively to Selkirk's plea, but his response was swift and unrelenting. He would brook no compromise. He turned him down flat. "There's no room for you on this ship . . ."

As he stood alone on the beach and watched the ship depart, tears filled Selkirk's eyes and spilled down his cheeks. This can't be happening, he thought, the man must have a heart. Come back!

But the ship slipped farther and farther away.

Selkirk plunged desperately into the sea and swam after the ship, but no one so much as lowered a rope for him to grab onto.

It was hopeless.

He was stranded on the deserted island, all alone.

I left the hotel with Allan Jardine and went to see the house where Selkirk was born. The Crusoe Hotel was built next to the wharf in Largo Bay, and the street extending east from there, called Main Street, ran alongside the firth. That part of town still looks much the way it did in the latter half of the seventeenth century, when Selkirk lived there. Even the faces of the old men walking slowly past the stone houses seemed to give a hint of the past. As we strolled through those surroundings where time stood still, I felt as if the lively scamp Alexander Selkirk might come tumbling out of any of the houses along the way.

Listening carefully, I could hear the sound of waves washing the Largo beach, crashing on it again and again—a sound unchanged from Selkirk's time.

Then there it was, the house where Selkirk was born.

Apparently it had been rebuilt some two hundred years after his birth, yet with its orange tiles and doors painted red and yellow, this stone house on Largo's Main Street appeared sufficiently old to me. And there, built into the center of the front wall on the second floor, was a statue of a rugged-looking man, his right hand shading his eyes as he looked out to sea. His hat, jacket, trousers, and shoes were all made of goatskin; at his waist hung a pistol and a sword, and in his left hand he held a musket. After years of exposure to rain and fog, the statue was coated with a patina, silent testimony to Selkirk's patience on the island as year after year he scanned the horizon for signs of a ship.

At the base of the statue was carved the year of its erection, 1885. Below that was a copper plate bearing the following inscription:

IN MEMORY OF ALEXANDER SELKIRK, MARINER, THE ORIGINAL OF ROBINSON CRUSOE WHO LIVED ON THE ISLAND OF JUAN FERNANDEZ IN COMPLETE SOLITUDE FOR FOUR YEARS AND FOUR MONTHS, HE DIED 1723,[5] LEUITENANT [SIC] OF H.M.S. WEYMOUTH AGED 47 YEARS. THIS STATUE IS ERECTED BY DAVID GILLIES, NET MANUFACTURER, ON THE SITE OF THE COTTAGE IN WHICH SELKIRK WAS BORN.

David Gillies, the person who erected the statue, turned out to be Allan Jardine's great-grandfather.

As I stood for a while looking up at the statue, taking in the expression on its face and its general appearance, I felt a sudden pang of surprise and joy, as if I had stumbled upon a man whom I should never by rights have been able to meet.

"What do you say, want to come in? There might be something else inside I could show you."

Following Jardine's beckoning, I stepped over the threshold into a white-walled apartment.

"When my father was still alive, this flat was kept up as a little museum. Selkirk's possessions aren't here any more . . ."

"What sort of possessions?"

"His musket."

---

5. The correct year of Selkirk's death is 1721. The log of the *H.M.S. Weymouth* is located in the London Public Record Office, and I was able to verify that he died on December 13, 1721 (see chapter 6, p. 157).

"The very one he used on the island?"

"Aye. But it would take a lot of looking to find it, that's what my father always said. It was auctioned off in London, you see, and then sold to someone in America, they say."

Entering into Allan Jardine's room, I found it to be made up like an artist's studio. It was not at all hard to imagine it as a privately run museum displaying Selkirk's belongings.

Jardine went and fetched some photographs to show me. In one of them, he was a small boy playing the bagpipes before an assemblage of village dignitaries at the museum's opening ceremony. As I studied the photograph, he seemed to remember something.

"Oh, aye. Why don't I play the bagpipes for you here? When I visited Selkirk's island in 1983, I set up a monument on the hill he used to climb up to search for a ship that would rescue him, and I played the bagpipes there in his memory. I don't have much occasion to play any more, but today is special."

With that he took out a set of well-used bagpipes from a black leather case and vigorously inflated the bag with air. Then he played a slow, pure melody, skillfully working the melody pipes and drone pipes. It was a traditional Scottish air, the melody of the hymn "Amazing Grace."

That night, Allan and I went back to the bar at The Crusoe Hotel and did some serious drinking. We would fill a whisky glass with one of the local single-malt whiskies, Haig or Cameron Brick, and knock it back in one gulp. Those very dry liquors left an acrid taste in the mouth. We would drink a chaser of lager beer, and then start all over again.

Along the way other villagers joined in, and we sang and carried on. Over and over I told them my next dream, to explore Robinson Crusoe Island in the South Pacific. Every time I talked about my plan, Allan would explain to everyone how beautiful the sea was when he visited the island and how many birds there were. He looked very happy when he talked about it. Villagers who had looked on me with curiosity at first now came up to slap me on the back and offer encouragement. We were all enjoying the moment.

The villagers were rustic and shy, yet fine-spirited and generous. When I matched them drink for drink, their ordinary taciturnity and reserve seemed to drop away, letting me catch a glimpse of a side of them normally kept under wraps.

Morose to all appearances, they were in fact as cheerful and gracious as could be. As I looked on the men of Largo, I thought of Selkirk, born and raised in this place, and I felt my image of him take on flesh and resonance.

Before I knew it, the sky was growing light with dawn. Hungover as I was, I dragged myself out to see Selkirk's statue one more time. Drenched in morning sunshine, it shone brilliantly. Today again he was looking out to sea, one hand over his eyes.

I too stared at the horizon. Beyond it lay the island I would seek.

CHAPTER Three

Robinson Crusoe Island

My shocked expression said it all: Was I really going to get in this thing?

I was at the Aeropuerto Los Cerrillos in Santiago, Chile, standing in front of the Cessna 320, the plane that would fly me to Robinson Crusoe Island, the present name of Mas-a-Tierra in the Juan Fernandez Archipelago. I had already been told that this model only seated five, but now that I could actually see the plane, it looked so untrustworthy that I choked.

A walk from nose to tail would take barely three good strides, the wings were paper-thin and short, and the noise of the propeller was no louder than a mosquito's hum, wherever I stood. And the man who introduced himself to me in a gravelly voice as a seasoned pilot was bent double with old age.

"*Buenos dias, señor!*" He greeted me with supreme confidence and flashed a guileless smile that revealed a set of yellowed teeth. Then he asked point-blank, "How much do you weigh?" When I was slow to reply, he repeated impatiently, "What's your weight in kilograms?"

I told him, and the old man responded by reaching inside his pouch and pulling out a scale that he set on the ground in front of me. "Put your bag on there. That big back-pack you've got, set it on the scale." I hoisted my backpack on the scale, and instantly his expression darkened. "Twenty-five kilos [fifty-five pounds]. Not good."

"I beg your pardon?"

"You know something? Only the first ten kilos of luggage is free. After that, it costs you 1,000 pesos per kilo."

Seeing my horrified expression, the old man seemed to have a change of heart. Perhaps he decided it was not fair to fleece a young fellow traveling all alone. Chuckling gently, he said, "Never mind, today it's all right. I charge you nothing. It's free."

The pilot went on to explain that if the plane were overloaded it would crash, and if the weight was not distributed just right, it would wobble dangerously. He then went around asking all five passengers their weights and assigning seats on that basis; then he weighed every piece of luggage to decide just where it would be stowed. The situation made me smile hugely until I remembered that I would actually be flying over the Pacific in this contraption—and I sobered up immediately.

"Is this really going to be safe?" I wondered aloud.

Today was December 24, 1994. Christmas Eve. Here in the southern hemisphere it was midsummer, and even at 10:00 A.M. Santiago was boiling, with the temperature over 30° C [86° F]. The concrete underfoot seemed to absorb the heat and gave off waves of hot air. Now and then a dry wind blew, causing the far-off horizon to shimmer and leaves on the trees to reflect back the burning light. This was certainly a different kind of Christmas Eve than the ones I'd been used to.

Despite my misgivings, I climbed aboard the fragile-looking Cessna 320, squeezed into the narrow seat, and strapped myself into place with the wide seat belt. The plane was used both by tourists and by the islanders themselves for getting to and from the mainland; I decided that two of my fellow passengers looked like islanders. When all was ready, the pilot took his place in the cockpit and began clicking an assortment of switches into the "on" position. The propeller began to revolve, and the plane rolled forward, taxiing onto the runway. We came to a complete stop, and then permission for liftoff came from the control tower. The engine was revved up to full throttle and we began hurtling down the runway.

Dear God, may we please not crash. . . .

Up in the cockpit, our pilot was totally relaxed. He turned around and grinned at me, flashing those yellow teeth.

We were off to Robinson Crusoe Island. My twenty-five-kilo backpack and I had taken the first step on our big adventure.

Once the air currents stabilized, I could see nothing but the beautiful ocean below and my fears evaporated. I

succumbed to the illusion that we were being sucked on-
ward by some invisible power. For a while, I dozed.

The next thing I knew, over three hours had passed and
the plane had started to lose altitude, the propeller zero-
ing in on the bit of brownish land visible on the horizon
ahead.

This was it. The island I had spent so much time trying
to imagine was now about to become a reality.

At my first glimpse of it, I had to catch my breath. There
were sheer cliffs, desolate rock walls that threatened to
pulverize our little aircraft in an instant if we should so
much as brush against them. The island wore a much
more forbidding look than I had ever imagined.

On the western side, there was a tiny patch of flat land
resembling a gray lunar surface that turned out to be the
landing strip. As we flew over it, the old man at the con-
trols banked sharply and prepared to land.

The Juan Fernandez Archipelago in the South Pacific,
some 670 kilometers [about 416 miles] off the coast of
Chile, is a scattering of three tiny islands. Formed millions
of years ago by underwater volcanic eruptions, the islands
are inhospitable not only because of their steep, precipitous mountains but also because they are so isolated, so
far from the South American mainland.

A Spanish seaman named Juan Fernandez discovered
the islands in 1574. Over the next two hundred years,
the largest of the three, Mas-a-Tierra (Spanish for "the
island closest to land"), which had a relatively flat natural harbor, became well known to sailors en route
across the Pacific as a good place to stop for food and
provisions, as well as lumber and firewood. Spanish
frigates bearing stolen Incan treasures back to Europe
moored there, as did pirate ships intent on plundering

those same frigates. Seal hunters from the north came down in search of new hunting grounds. Still, visits by humans remained rare, no more than one or two every few years.

The Spanish made periodic attempts at colonization. Time after time, a number of families would come to the islands, but developing and settling the archipelago proved an elusive goal. All known attempts ended in failure. Juan Fernandez himself attempted to transplant people from South America, but he failed to obtain government approval for his plan.

However, each wave of attempted immigration resulted in domestic animals like goats and cats being left behind, along with hardy plants. Such life forms thrived in isolation.

According to an account by the well-known buccaneer William Dampier, a member of the Moskito tribe found himself stranded on Mas-a-Tierra in 1681, twenty-three years before Alexander Selkirk. Known affectionately as "Will" aboard the English ship where he had been a sailor, the man lived for three years and two months on the island, armed only with a gun, a knife, a small powder flask made of horn, and a few bullets. He serrated the blade of the knife to make it into a saw and built himself a small hut some 800 meters [2625 feet] from shore. To catch fish, he fashioned a harpoon, barbs, and fishhooks; for a fishing line, he used leather rope made from strips of sealskin.

Will's abandonment and rescue both occurred during Dampier's thirteen-year-long sea voyage, which began in 1679 and ended in 1691. What is strange is that, on his very next outing (1703–7), Dampier commanded the expedition that saw Selkirk abandoned on the selfsame island, although he was not personally responsible for the incident. Dampier describes Will's rescue in the following words:

> *He saw our Ship the Day before we came to an Anchor, and did believe we were* English, *and therefore kill'd three Goats in the Morning, before we came to an Anchor, and drest them with Cabbage, to treat us when we came ashore. He came then to the Seaside to congratulate our safe Arrival. And when we landed, a* Moskito Indian, *named* Robin, *first leap'd ashore and running to his Brother* Moskito *Man, threw himself flat on his face at his feet, who helping him up, and embracing him, fell flat with his face on the Ground at* Robin's *feet, and was by him taken up also. We stood with pleasure to behold the surprize, and tenderness, and solemnity of this Interview, which was exceedingly affectionate on both Sides; and when their Ceremonies of Civility were over, we also that stood gazing at them drew near, each of us embracing him we had found here, who was overjoyed to see so many of his old Friends come hither, as he thought purposely to fetch him. He was named* Will, *as the other was* Robin. *These were names given them by the* English, *for they had no Names among themselves.*[1]

Will is said to have been the prototype for Friday, the other main character in Defoe's *Robinson Crusoe*. Long before Selkirk's arrival, the dramatic groundwork was being laid for one of the world's great novels.

As was true for Will, the abundant fresh water and edible plant and animal life on the island continued to be a lifeline for sailors on long voyages across the vast, faceless ocean. English sailors would later nickname the islands

---

1. William Dampier, *A New Voyage round the World* (New York: Dover Publications, 1968), p. 67.

"the Pacific Gibraltar." Just as the Straits of Gibraltar provided a reassuring landmark for mariners in the Mediterranean Sea, so the cluster of islands in the Pacific were an asylum where seafarers could be sure of their position and find rest.

At the end of the eighteenth century, Louis Antoine de Bougainville (1729–1811), a French navigator who explored unknown regions of the South Pacific on a voyage round the world, described the island as follows in his 1771 account *Voyage Autour du Monde* (*A Voyage Around the World*):

> *I intended to go to the Juan Fernandez Island and carry out astronomical observations. I hoped by that means to establish a definite starting-point for voyages across this vast ocean which is given such different indications of size by different seafarers. Now I was here to take my own chances on the island.*

When we landed at the airport—little more than a strip of barren land covered in red dirt—clouds of grasshoppers rose up simultaneously from the ground. Notwithstanding its grim appearance, the island clearly had sufficient nutrients to sustain enormous numbers of these creatures.

A gentle breeze blew in from the sea, and as soon as I had retrieved my backpack and thanked the pilot, who had grown in stature since my first appraisal, I headed off in the direction of that salt air. When I reached the shore, I found it was a boat landing; from there, my fellow passengers and I set off in a small diesel boat on a ninety-minute trip to the fishing village of San Juan Bautista.

Heading from the west to the northeast the boat clung to the edge of the island, put-putting its way along. I took

in sheer cliffs, waterfalls plunging straight down into the
sea from high overhead, and sharp, rocky reefs sticking
out of the water. As far as I could see, there was nowhere
to bring the boat close in, let alone a sandy beach where
people might go ashore. The island seemed a fortress rising all alone out of a far-off sea, forbidding and hostile.

By contrast, the skies were exhilaratingly blue and clear,
and the water was a deep, bright emerald. Against the
dark background of the cliffs, the wheeling petrels looked
all the whiter. I felt overwhelmed, yet strongly attracted.

The island of Mas-a-Tierra, now Robinson Crusoe Island, is shaped roughly like a boomerang. It is a tiny island 47.1 square kilometers [18.19 sq. miles] in area, the
size of the Island of Tiree in the Inner Hebrides. Even in
February, when the average temperature reaches its high
for the year, it is a mild 22° C [about 72° F]. Rarely does
the mercury top 30° C [86° F], it seems, and in winter, it
stays around 10° C [50° F].

For that reason, there is little point in dividing the year
into summer and winter. Rather, since seventy percent of
the island's annual rainfall is concentrated in the period
from April to October, it makes more sense to call that the
rainy season and the rest of the year the dry season. Annual rainfall is about 1,000 ml [61 cubic inches], approximately the same as the rainfall each year in New York
City. (London's average rainfall is 700 ml [41 cubic
inches] by comparison.)

The tallest peak on the island is El Yunque in the south,
measuring 915 meters [about 3000 feet] above sea level.
It is flanked on either side by a chain of mountains extending all across the center of the island. To the north is
gently rolling terrain that drops straight off into Cumberland Bay.

The climate is balmy year round and the cold water of the Humboldt Current, running north from Antarctica, means that the surrounding ocean teems with fish, which colonies of seals and storm petrels gather along the shore to catch. At times, depending on the direction of the wind, the predators' cries carry all the way to the primeval forests deep inland.

In these dense forests filled with luma trees and a kind of palm called chonta, brightly colored hummingbirds dart swiftly from flower to flower, giving off shrill cries as they dance wildly about.

For unimaginable eons, these islands knew no human presence. Like the Galapagos Islands and the Hawaiian Islands, this was a Garden of Eden where plant and animal life that had somehow crossed over from the mainland gradually adapted to its new environment and evolved.

The task I had set myself on this particular expedition was to locate the site of Alexander Selkirk's house. In his book *A Cruising Voyage round the World,* Selkirk's rescuer, Woodes Rogers, indicated that somewhere on the island where Selkirk had endured four years and four months of total isolation, rough accommodations had been constructed: "He built two Hutts with Piemento Trees, cover'd them with long Grass, and lin'd them with the Skins of Goats."

Assuming Selkirk had used those huts as his home base, finding remnants of them or their location would be a major step toward understanding his life there, shedding light on many mysteries. Which part of which island had he called home? How had he made the place habitable? The answers to these and other questions might be within reach. Perhaps by some miracle his house had even survived intact, untouched deep in a wooded corner of the island. After three hundred years, it would be in a state of utter dilapidation, in fact outright decay. Still, it was just possible that some trace of Selkirk would remain. None of the existing accounts offered the slightest clue as to the specific location of the lost settlement. My only hope was to work it out for myself. To live in any sort of comfort for four years and four months would require several *sine qua nons.* Defoe's novel *Robinson Crusoe* lists three: first, fresh water; second, protection from direct sunlight; and third, a clear view of the sea, to watch for ships that might bring deliverance. I had come up with an amended list of requirements:

1. *Proximity to fresh water.*
2. *Readily-available food.*
3. *Level ground.*
4. *Shelter from sun and rain.*
5. *Access to the sea—a nearby elevation providing an unobstructed view.*

In the months leading up to my trip, I went through Captain Rogers's account and note all references to the plants and animals that had figured in Selkirk's life.

I learned that Selkirk's huts were made of pimento wood and roofed with long grass. The goats found everywhere on the island played a crucial role in Selkirk's survival. He used their skins not only to cover the walls of the huts but also to make clothes, and he used the meat for food. On the beach were herds of seals and sea lions that he threaded his way around to go diving for lobsters.

Leaves of cabbage trees tasted like cabbage, as the name suggests, and other wild vegetables such as Sicilian radishes, turnips, and watercress are thought to have sprung up from seeds left by Westerners who dropped anchor at the island over the years. Records also indicated that Selkirk was plagued by rats and that he kept tame cats.

By going over a map of the island with all of these points in mind, I had significantly narrowed down the areas worth exploring. To my dismay, though, I discovered that obtaining a map of Robinson Crusoe Island was a tricky business. Whichever institution or map company I tried, the answer was the same: "Not in stock." Apparently, no detailed maps of the island existed. I did manage to obtain a few in greatly reduced scale, amounting to little more than a bean-sized outline in the middle of the ocean. It had never occurred to me that there might be unmapped corners of the earth in this day and age, but topographical maps with contour lines are published only if there is a demand for them. And this island was truly godforsaken.

Eventually, I decided to write a letter to the aerial photograph division of the Chilean Air Force and received word that they did indeed have aerial photographs taken for surveying purposes. However, no package from Chile had arrived by the time I left for my trip. The best guide I was able to find was an American marine chart giving a rough indication of the topographical features of the island.

I had done my best to figure out what conditions were necessary for Selkirk's huts, and I had assembled other clues as well, but I was unable to build on these conjectures to form any sort of detailed plan. Without a clear picture of the place where I was going, I could not decide what type of gear to take, from footwear on up. And even though the island was now inhabited, once I entered its hinterlands I would have to be self-sufficient. Whether I took a slingshot for catching birds or a pole for catching fish might very well mean the difference between life and death.

I was given an introduction to a man called Yuichi Watanabe, who, as a keen angler, sailed the world in a small fishing boat, joining up along the way with the novelist and passionate fisherman Takeshi Kaiko to go fishing in Scotland.

I showed him my U.S. marine chart, and asked his opinion of the type of fish I would be likely to catch. The map showed thirteen rivers like cracks on the island, emerging from convoluted ravines. Even if they all varied in their width, length, water volume, and speed of current, any large river would have a good chance of containing freshwater fish. Based on that assumption, Watanabe presented me with a light, portable fishing rod complete with hooks and line, as well as some flies in case I had no luck in catching river insects for bait.

It was in 1750, half a century after Alexander Selkirk left the island, that the Spaniards founded the village of San Juan Bautista, with an eye to claiming this excellent harbor. The current population is approximately seven hundred.

As we drew near, the villagers and their children formed a crowd around the boat landing in the harbor, showering smiles on me, a total stranger. They were white-skinned, and I realised that they must be descendants of settlers from Spain and Chile.

"*Buenos tardes!*" I called to them as I climbed out of the boat and headed into the village.

For the whole day and night, I could hear nothing but the whoosh and boom of waves; the village is entirely surrounded by the sound of the sea. In the center of the town is a plaza where people gather to relax, and alongside it is the main street. Barely 200 meters [656 feet] long, this gravel road connects to every path in San Juan Bautista and is the great artery of village life. A clinic, a police station, a harbor office, a mini-market, a post office, a gymnasium, a soccer field, a cemetery, private houses—village buildings and sites are scattered unevenly across the level land, but everything faces the sea.

Almost everyone in town is a fisherman. Most of the local income comes from *langosta*, or lobsters, which are prized for their flavor thanks to the cold ocean current. Gourmets cannot get enough of the rich, succulent flesh, and orders pour in from the mainland. The price is not cheap, either.

When lobsters aren't in season, there is little else the island can offer, so the villagers are forced to earn a whole year's income during a few months. All summer long, the fishermen's eyes are steely with determination, yet their eyes never seem to lose their sparkle. And apart from a certain bashfulness in both children and adults, the islanders love to laugh. The moment I saw their smiles, I stopped feeling nervous about living in this strange outpost.

This tiny village would be the starting point for my expedition, and it would be the ending-point as well.

In spite of my eagerness to find what might remain of Selkirk's huts, I knew that I couldn't simply plunge recklessly into the thicket, relying solely on my own hunches to guide me. The quality and efficiency of my exploration depended on how skillfully I could elicit and analyze information from the islanders. They had lived there for generations, and anything they might teach me would doubtless prove very valuable.

Getting to know the villagers and building mutual trust could be accomplished to a certain extent without words. But to convey my immediate aim, not to mention my passion and my dream, would be difficult unless I could communicate verbally. I had learned a little Spanish in preparation for the trip, but when the conversation became the slightest bit complicated I was unable to convey my own thoughts, nor did I have the least idea what the other person was saying. Terrible misunderstandings might easily occur. Moreover, my memory often failed me at crucial moments.

Anticipating that this would be a problem, before leaving I had thought about what I would most likely need to say, and I had gotten a Spanish-speaking friend to translate it for me. The result bore no resemblance to ordinary conversation guidebooks. Its peculiar content caused even my friend to smile, but at last my own personal Spanish bible was complete. It went something like this:

Phrase one: "No soy nada sospechoso." *(I am not a suspicious character.)*

Phrase two: "Vengo aqui a hacer una encuesta sobre las huellas de Alejandro Selkirk." *(I have come here to study traces of the life of Alexander Selkirk.)*

Phrase three: "¿Quedan vestigos de los habitantes de la antiguedad remota?" *(Are there any vestiges of human habitation from long ago?)*

With this phrasebook in hand, I patiently entered into dialogue with the islanders. The response was disappointing. "I don't know." "Sorry." "Never heard of anything." Accepting such answers as inevitable, I spoke to children as well as adults. It occurred to me that an old hut might make a fine secret playground. But as it turned out, no one knew anything about an old hut or huts that might have belonged to Alexander Selkirk. After three hundred years, the possibility of there being traces of his life on the island was utterly remote from people's consciousness; an event so buried in the past had nothing whatsoever to do with their daily lives.

There was, however, one boy who was able to show me a place with signs of ancient human habitation. The children's playground was in a cave in the side of a mountain behind the village. Known familiarly as Cueva de los Patriotas or Patriots' Cave, this was where Chilean insurrectionists once lived after being sentenced to exile during Chile's war of independence from Spain. Inside the dark, dank cave, the anguish of those convicts from the early 1800s seemed to linger undiminished. The cave walls were green with moss, and a big chunk was cut away where a statue of the Virgin Mary had once stood. A network of tunnels that connected the main cave with others had survived intact.

Smiling and eager in spite of our communication difficulties, the child also took me to a forest called Plazaleta El Yunque. During the First World War, remnants of the crew of the German battleship *Dresden* had managed to make their way to the island after their ship was blown up and sunk by the British; the stone foundations of a house they had built could still be seen. The men all lived out the remainder of their lives on the island and apparently became known in their home country as the "German Crusoes." They were buried on the north side of the village in the public cemetery, where there was also a cenotaph to all the soldiers who had perished at sea.

The more I learned, the more apparent it became that the island—home to exiles, castaways, people struggling to survive—had a peculiar and checkered history, both before and after Selkirk's time. Were all trips to the island ill-fated? Was my own journey doomed?

The sites the boy had shown me were at least a starting point: the area around both the hillside caves and the stone house afforded excellent views, without being too conspicuous. They were surrounded by trees but had sufficient sunshine as well; on sweltering afternoons, there was a pleasant combination of shade and filtered light. Both were located midway up hills, on level and comfortable ground. The availability of water was an open question, but both sites seemed to offer many amenities. I would have to get a really good sense of the lay of the land and the environment before I could possibly hope to pinpoint the spot where Selkirk had elected to build his huts.

The only place on the island that is known to be directly connected to Selkirk is the central elevation known in English as Selkirk's Lookout, and to the villagers as El Mirador. It stands 565 meters [1854 feet] above sea level. Today, there is a well-traveled path from the village of San Juan Bautista to Selkirk's Lookout. The path travels down the gentle slope behind the village plaza and through a valley, zigzags across mountain ridges, and then meanders up: to walk the entire distance takes about one hour. It is a small, natural lookout formed by the conjunction of two steep slopes and affording a good view of both the east and southwest sides of the island. There is no other place like it. Selkirk climbed up here daily, scanning the horizon for any sign of a ship that might bring rescue.

Two small monuments stand unobtrusively on this elevation overlooking the sea. One contains this inscription:

IN MEMORY OF ALEXANDER SELKIRK, MARINER,

A NATIVE OF LARGO, IN THE COUNTY OF FIFE, SCOT-LAND.

WHO LIVED ON THIS ISLAND IN COMPLETE SOLITUDE, FOR FOUR YEARS AND FOUR MONTHS.

HE WAS LANDED FROM THE CINQUE PORTS GALLEY, 96 TONS, 16 GUNS, A.D. 1704, AND WAS TAKEN OFF IN THE DUKE, PRIVATEER, 12TH FEB, 1709.

HE DIED LIEUTENANT OF H.M.S. WEYMOUTH, A.D.1723,[2] AGED 47 YEARS.

THIS TABLET IS ERECTED NEAR SELKIRK'S LOOKOUT, BY COMMODORE POWELL AND THE OFFICERS OF H.M.S. TOPAZE, A.D.1868.

Next to this rusted plate is a small monument in gray stone, with these words:

---

2. As previously indicated, his death actually occurred in 1721, at age forty-four.

TABLET PLACED HERE BY
ALLAN JARDINE
OF LARGO, FIFE, SCOTLAND
DIRECT DESCENDANT OF
ALEXANDER SELKIRK'S BROTHER DAVID
REMEMBRANCE
"TILL A' THE SEAS GANG DRY
AND THE ROCKS MELT IN THE
SUN" JANUARY 1983

I tried to imagine myself in Selkirk's place. If I were cast away on an uninhabited island, what would I do first?

Probably the first thing I would do would be to walk around and see if there was any danger, check for a water supply, and hunt for something to eat. After that, I'd probably look for a good place to sleep, either a cave or a clump of trees offering safe shelter. Once I had secured my safety and a food supply, as well as a comfortable place to be, I would want to explore my surroundings and find out what sort of a place I was in. Instinctively, I would probably climb up somewhere high to try to get a view of the island as a whole.

Selkirk's Lookout was the perfect place to check on one's surroundings. True, it was swept all day long by strong winds, but standing there one could see not only the island but also any ships on the horizon. According to the evidence offered in the written accounts and the testimony of both his descendants and the islanders that he had indeed climbed up here every day to search for rescue, Selkirk's main foothold on the island simply had to be nearby.

The lookout point commanded views to the east and southwest, and on both sides were gentle hills that would provide level ground with access to river water. The eastern side, known as Cumberland, was the most inviting area on the island, as the presence of the village San Juan

Bautista showed. The southwestern Villagra region was less hilly, but the view from Selkirk's Lookout made plain that the farther west one went, the more extensive patches of brown earth became, with only a small portion of terrain covered in dense vegetation.

After gazing from Selkirk's Lookout across the valleys that fell away on either side, I established satellite contact using a portable global positioning system (GPS) receiver, and gauged the exact position of the point: latitude 32°38'14.3" S, longitude 78°51'00.4" W. As I was jotting down the measurements, a man suddenly appeared on the mountain path, coming my way. He was a forest ranger with the Corporation National Forestal (CONAF). Pointing to my receiver, he began rattling away in vigorous Spanish, evidently up in arms about something.

Apparently I was being taken for a spy.

The island was designated as a national park and, except for in residential San Juan Bautista, walking around without permission was forbidden. Before I could go into the forest, I would have to apply for permission from the authorities.

No longer able to wander around as freely as I would have liked, I would have to put together a plan for my explorations, submit it to CONAF, and receive formal permission to carry on. From my conversations with villagers, and from my own observations so far, I was able to narrow my focus to three areas, Puerto Inglés, Villagra, and Cumberland.

Zone A: Puerto Inglés

As I listened carefully to the villagers, I learned of the existence of a cave steeped in legend, located on the northwest part of the island, on the shore of a bay called Puerto Inglés. It had at some point become known to the locals as Cueva de Robinson Crusoe, or Robinson Crusoe's Cave. I decided to make detailed observations of the cave and try to trek inland from there.

Zone B: Villagra

This area stretching southwest from Selkirk's Lookout had a river and gently rolling hills, perfectly fulfilling the requirements I had worked out for a suitable place to live. Since this part of the island remained untouched, there was a fair chance Selkirk's huts might still be standing if he had lived here.

Zone C: Cumberland

This was both the likeliest of the three zones to contain the site I was looking for and the most unlikely to yield tangible evidence. Land in the vicinity of the village had already undergone considerable development. The one area that remained untouched was the inland forest around Selkirk's Lookout, which I resolved to explore.

Having worked out my plan, I presented myself at the small barracks housing CONAF headquarters, seeking a permit to explore the island. The branch in charge of Robinson Crusoe Island was run by eleven people: the director, Mauricio Calderon, nine forest rangers, and one secretary. Most of their work consisted of tramping up and down the mountains doing field surveys.

In the late nineteenth and early twentieth centuries, the island was the focus of scientific study for natural scientists like Swedish botanist Carl Skottsberg (1880–1963), who established that approximately one-third of island flora was indigenous and could be found nowhere else on earth. In 1935 the entire Juan Fernandez Archipelago was designated a Chilean national park and later nominated as a forest preserve of the United Nations Educational, Scientific and Cultural Organization (UNESCO).

Mauricio Calderon had a mustache and thick eyebrows suggesting a strong will, and he looked somewhat younger than his forty years. His open expression revealed both intelligence and kindness. We quickly became friends and, because he spoke excellent English, I was able to discuss my plans and expectations with him in greater detail than I'd anticipated.

From the point of view of nature preservation, I was certainly a pest. Every time I entered the forest, grasses underfoot would be trampled, and if I camped out for any length of time, I would produce garbage and light fires. One by one, I showed him my heavy equipment: my portable cartridge-style gas cooking stove, my candle lantern, and my headlamp. I assured him that I had no intention of building any bonfires, and I swore fervently that I would bring back all my garbage with me. It crossed my mind that despite its name, Robinson Crusoe Island must be one of the hardest places in the world to become a Robinson Crusoe today.

Eventually, my assurances that I would carry out my exploration as responsibly as possible won Calderon over, and he issued the necessary permit. It consisted of a single sheet of paper with a single sentence, which he dashed off on the spot. Translated, it would read:

> *I hereby grant permission to Daisuke Takahashi from Japan to enter the national park.*
> > *CONAF Regional Director*
> > *Mauricio Calderon*

He then offered me these words of encouragement: "This island is named after Robinson Crusoe, but there are still all kinds of things we don't know about his prototype, Selkirk."

We exchanged a firm handshake, and I found myself trembling with eagerness. Now it was off into the wild, all alone—the start of my life as Robinson Crusoe.

CHAPTER

Four

The Search

Zone A: Puerto Inglés

I spotted one of the village fishermen walking back from the port one day. Seizing the opportunity, I showed him the chart and asked him in my faltering Spanish whether he would take me to Puerto Inglés the next day. "*Si, por supuesto,*" he replied, in his laid-back manner, but I wasn't completely sure that he had understood and so I was pleasantly surprised to find him waiting for me by his boat the next morning.

Located some two and a half kilometers [about one and a half miles] northwest from San Juan Bautista,

Puerto Inglés is a rare natural harbor on this cliff-bound island. Though the harbor is only a fifteen-minute boat ride from the village, getting there by foot would have taken all day—an indication of the island's severe terrain.

Also called Little Bay or Baia del Oeste (West Bay), Puerto Inglés is known to mariners as that rarity, an ocean harbor with a river, yet to this day no one lives there or plans to develop the area. Viewed from the sea, the shore is gently curving and strewn with big black rocks. Inland there are jostling hills with narrow valleys that penetrate deep into the interior.

As we got closer, I saw trees growing along the rocky shoreline in a distinctive V shape, clearly planted that way by some human hand. I got out of the boat and the fisherman handed me my heavy backpack, his sun-burned face breaking into a smile of understanding as I asked him to come back in ten days to pick me up. Then he left, and I was alone.

Standing and watching the boat disappear from view, I felt a total calmness steal over me. At the same time, I felt apprehensive: would I really be able to pull this off? The island wasn't uninhabited anymore—but even so, for the next ten days I'd be entirely on my own.

At around 9:00 P.M., the sun sank behind the mountains, the wind took on a chill, and the blue of the sky deepened. I faced my first night alone. After putting up my tent outside the entrance to Robinson Crusoe's Cave, I went to get water from a nearby stream. The water shone clear, reflecting the color of the sky. The moment I set foot on the bank, a black cloud of grasshoppers jumped into the air and landed on the blue surface of the water. Overhead, wispy clouds rode across the dark mountains, flying over the majestic scene. The stream in front of me came tumbling down from those mountain depths and I scooped up some water in my hands and drank. It tasted pure and sweet.

I soon filled my canteen and set about making dinner. The provisions I had brought with me included 2 kilos [4.4 pounds] of rice, consommé cubes, salt, pepper, curry powder, chocolate bars, and vitamins. That was all.

I lit my portable gas cooking stove, and a bright blue flame sprang up in the gathering dusk. Ten minutes later, the enticing smell of cooking rice rose in the air. I let it cook a few minutes extra to scorch the bottom of the rice a little, the way I like it. Then I switched off the fire and sat down for my first solitary meal on the island: white rice and consommé. As dinners go it wasn't much, but considering the circumstances, it was a banquet.

When it got so dark that I could no longer make out my surroundings, I lit the candle in my lantern and crawled into the tent. The candle flame swayed in the breeze, setting my shadow dancing around the walls of my tent.

Night on the island was cool and comfortable, with none of the lingering steaminess of continental nights in the tropics. I scribbled some notes and impressions in my diary, until my eyes felt heavy.

However, the minute I lay down and closed my eyes, I began to hear all sorts of noises I hadn't heard before. Was that the tide coming in? Waves crashed onto the beach with surprising force, moving stones around or carrying them out to sea, making a racket like the end of the world. As I lay stretched out on the ground, it felt like the stones were heading my way. I could hear them getting closer. A tsunami of stones. *Damn. Why didn't I remember about the tide? If I'm going to get up and move, better do it* now. These thoughts raced through my brain until finally I jumped up and stuck my head out the tent flap. Of course, absolutely nothing had altered.

I calmed myself and got back into my sleeping bag. This time, it wasn't long before I began to hear cries of some unfamiliar beast. What on earth could it be? Utterly alone in a strange place, I lay sleepless inside my tent, beads of cold sweat forming on my forehead. While up, I'd heard nothing, but now the animal seemed to be lurking just outside my tent. What the hell was going on? *There it goes again. What'll I do? What do I do? Burst outside, yelling my head off? Better play it safe—think now, where'd that hatchet go?* My mind reeled with half-formed thoughts. I was excited, on edge. Finally, unable to stand it any more, I leaped up and stuck my head outside.

To my disbelief, there was no sign of any animal, let alone a predator. The surroundings lay still and unchanged. Waves kept up their rhythmic pounding, dragging stones in their wake. Between rifts in the clouds now covering the sky, here and there a white star shone.

Cold air poured in through the tent opening as I got out a bottle of Scotch (which I'd brought for emergencies . . .) and took a big swig, feeling the warmth spread down inside me. I reflected on what a lot I'd discovered in one day: not just the strength and smell of the wind or the size, color, and shape of rocks along the shore, but the way people had once lived here and the kinds of tension they must have felt. . . . The minute I found myself alone in Puerto Inglés, all this information came to me. Yet that wasn't quite right, either. The sounds of the waves and stones, the mysterious animal cries—they hadn't entered me so much as *I* had entered *them*. What was so scary about a few unfamiliar sounds, anyway? By tomorrow they'd seem normal. Telling myself this, I felt my uneasiness dispel.

Robinson Crusoe had been terrified on his first night too:

> *Night coming upon me, I began with a heavy heart to consider what would be my lot if there were any ravenous beasts in that country, seeing at night they always come abroad for their prey.*
>
> *All the remedy that offered to my thoughts at that time was to get up into a thick bushy tree like a firr, but thorny, which grew near me, and where I resolved to sit all night, and consider the next day what death I should dye, for as yet I saw no prospect of life; I walked about a furlong from the shore, to see if I could find any fresh water to drink, which I did, to my great joy; and having drank, and put a little tobacco in my mouth to prevent hunger, I went to the tree, and getting up into it, endeavoured to place myself so, as that if I should sleep I might not fall; and having cut me a short stick, like a truncheon, for my defence, I took up my lodging, and having been excessively fatigued, I fell first asleep and slept as comfortably as, I believe, few could have done in my condition, and found my self the most refreshed with it that I think I ever was on such an occasion.[1]*

In the morning, I started exploring as soon as I'd eaten breakfast. The legendary cave of Robinson Crusoe was of course the most intriguing site, one that would require careful examination—yet what surprised me about Puerto Inglés was the presence of other signs of previous human habitation clustered near the ocean. When or by whom they had been made, I couldn't tell.

---

1. Daniel Defoe, *Robinson Crusoe* (New York: Penguin Classics, 1985), pp. 66–67.

The bay stretched out to the east and west, with Robinson Crusoe's Cave quite far to the east. From there, looking westward, I could see a patchwork of level grasslands and sterile stony ground, the V-shaped wedge of large trees, and a small stream. The western end of the shore was cut off by Cerro Alto, a 650-meter [2133-foot] mountain with signs of human habitation concentrated at its foot.

I decided to begin my exploration in Robinson Crusoe's Cave, a natural wind-carved hollow in rock that was once lava from an underground volcano. Four or five meters [thirteen to sixteen feet] high, the entrance looked out onto the sea; it was barricaded with dozens of crossed sticks, evidently the remnant of a windscreen built long ago. Inside, the cave was not very deep, barely offering protection from the elements. A number of niches were cut into the innermost wall—perfect places to build a fire or put cooking utensils. What interested me most of all was the knee-high stone enclosure built around the cave: neat piles of stones lay in an area twenty meters [sixty-six feet] square, creating a clearly demarcated boundary.

The sight reminded me of Robinson Crusoe's dwelling as Defoe describes it in the novel. His tent pitched on "a little plain on the side of a rising hill," Crusoe then "drew a half circle before the hollow place which took in about ten yards in its semi-diameter from the rock, and twenty yards in its diameter." He then pitched two rows of stakes along that half circle, adding others inside them at an angle to make a secure fence within which he set up his tent and carried all his stores. The setup before my eyes was virtually identical with the one in the book.

In front of the cave was a faded sign erected by the Corporation National Forestal (CONAF) to the effect that Selkirk had lived here for four years and four months. The sign certainly gave credence to the theory—and yet Calderon had said nothing about it. Was there any truth to this claim?

My gut instinct said not. It seemed just too good to be true. I strongly suspected that someone had deliberately put up this fence based on Defoe's description; but in order to be sure, I would have to suppress my doubts and take a good look around. For one thing, there were those indications of later habitation; others had perhaps been encouraged to settle here by finding traces of a predecessor—a previous inhabitant that could well have been Alexander Selkirk.

First, in front of the stone fence on a small sandy spot overlooking the sea, there were two rusted ancient cannons, each about a meter and a half [five feet] long, one half-buried in sand. No sign of cannonballs or battery.

Second, at the foot of Cerro Alto on the western side of the bay, I found what was left of four stone houses, a livestock pen, and a small, white stone chapel. Three of the ruins stood in a row near the sea, and the other was further inland by a stream. All were in such a state of dilapidation that they gave little indication of how the original buildings may have looked. From the foundations I made out the location of the entrance to each house and saw that the larger ones had two rooms. The wooden livestock pen, located behind the row of three houses, was large enough to hold five or six horses or cows. It was firmly planted in the ground, and with a little repair it would still have been quite serviceable.

The chapel, meanwhile, gave me a strong sense of the settlers' state of mind. In their lonely existence on this island, undisturbed by visitors, what had those devout Christians prayed for? They had lived simply, with only domestic animals and one another for company; now their statue of the Virgin Mary was in a pitiful state of disrepair, the head fallen off and missing, with no one to set it to rights. I did what I could, gathering wild-flowers and placing them before the headless statue in offering.

As I retraced the history of the island, I understood better the role of the settlers and also the reason this natural harbor was named Puerto Inglés—"English Port." Spanish colonists had built a fort here from which to launch attacks on marauding English pirates. The ruins showed where those whose job it was to protect the fort would have lived.

In the seventeenth and eighteenth centuries, European mariners knew of this harbor as a sanctuary in the open seas. As a source of fresh water and provisions, however, it definitely took a back seat to Cumberland Bay on the eastern side of the island, which is much larger and more accommodating, with plenty of space for two ships to lie at anchor and for two hundred crewmen to stretch their legs and fill their bellies. Puerto Inglés could not compete.

Whether the *Cinque Portes* had abandoned Alexander Selkirk at Cumberland Bay or at Puerto Inglés is unclear. Without the log for the voyage, there is no longer any way of knowing. What I *was* sure of was that Selkirk would have built his house within easy reach of the lookout point he walked to each day. Was there a direct route from here to Selkirk's Lookout, I wondered?

Puerto Inglés is a gentle, fan-shaped valley, with a river wending its way down from rolling hills. The harbor faces due north and is enclosed by mountains some 500 or 600 meters [about 1640 to 1969 feet] above sea level: Cerro Agudo on the south, Cerro Portezuelo on the southeast, and Cerro Alto on the west. According to my map, Selkirk's Lookout lay just beyond the central peak of Portezuelo. If I could cross that peak and find a trail to the lookout, the possibility that Selkirk had lived in this seaside cave would seem stronger.

Of course I had to keep in mind the other five requirements besides the existence of a trail: fresh water, a source of food, flat ground, sunshine, and a view of the sea. I began by following the river inland in a southwesterly direction until it divided at the foot of Cerro Portezuelo, one tributary coming from the east, one from the west. Their juncture became the focus of my exploration. I named the river the Puerto Inglés River and dubbed its tributaries East River and West River. My trek across the 550-meter [1804-foot] Cerro Portezuelo in search of Selkirk's trail would start here.

This being the dry season, the deciduous trees of the forest had all shed their leaves, exposing long, bare branches that wound around each other in complex patterns. Here and there they formed natural tunnels or dense walls that blocked the way. Elsewhere they looked something like rough hovels, stirring false hopes in me again and again.

The leaves underfoot formed a deep, soft carpet. Everywhere I went I came upon large fallen trees like beautiful abstract objets d'art. On the upper slopes, big broadleafed trees put out a bright canopy of new leaves through which cool rays of sunlight fell, dappling the ground at my feet. The forest was solemnly still, as if it had been that way forever.

Since I spent the greater part of every day climbing mountains and hiking, more than anything else I looked forward to getting back to my tent every night and cooking a hot dinner. Just planning the menu and how I would prepare it gave me a lift. At the same time, I worried constantly about how I was going to supplement my Spartan diet. The Puerto Inglés River was actually little more than a trickle—no hope of catching any tadpoles there, let alone fish. All the fishing equipment I had lugged with me appeared to be useless.

In the rocks I came across some tiny crabs, but they scampered away so fast that catching any seemed impossible. I gave it my best shot, but in the end I had to give up. There didn't seem to be any edible wildlife on the shore. I was in trouble.

Or was I? After a little thought, I decided to try sea fishing. I took out a lure I'd brought along in case bait was scarce, fastened it to my fishing line, and dropped it in the sea—but nothing happened. It was made for river fish, so to ocean fish it must have looked like an odd bit of floating matter, not dinner. I decided to get back to basics and follow the angler's golden rule: *use what the fish usually eat as bait.*

I thought back to those great swarms of grasshoppers by the river. Every time I went to get water they would jump up in a cloud, some of them inevitably falling into the stream, which then carried them out to sea. On a breezy day, even more rode out to sea on gusts of wind. If there were any fish near the island, perhaps they were feeding on grasshoppers. I decided to try using one as bait. If the fish showed interest, my worries would be over.

Catching the insects was child's play. I would chase one into the water, pick it up and, yes, I admit this was cruel, pluck off its wings and its legs. In scarcely five minutes I had captured a dozen and set off to try my luck. Warmed by the afternoon sun, the sea lay calm before me. Worth a try at least, I thought. Would fish really eat grasshoppers? I had no idea. Even assuming they would, would the fish themselves then be palatable? More to the point, *were* there any fish in these waters?

I stared at the end of my line. To my amazement, there was an immediate tug. The next thing I knew, the pole bent in a huge arc, and the tip began turning around and around on the surface of the water. The pull was not overly strong, but the pole danced in my hands with so much energy and life that I was afraid I might lose my grip. In terms of sheer physical strength there was no contest between me and whatever I had snagged, but it put up such a fierce and spirited fight that I began to feel like the underdog.

The struggle went on for some time, but eventually the fish seemed to exhaust itself, the line going slack. Now it was my turn. I seized the chance to pull as hard as I could, attempting to drag my prize to the surface, but the fish promptly redoubled its efforts to get away. Again, the pole bent sharply as the fish made a last-ditch surge. Afraid that the pole might snap in two, I eased up—and immediately the fish made a run for it. I stopped trying to lift the pole and instead drew it along sideways. The fish strove to swim in the opposite direction, but after a while I wore it down. Slowly I raised the end of the pole, and below me the fish's silver belly flashed like a knife in the water.

With one swift gesture I yanked up the rod, the water parted with a splash, and the soaked line and hook landed at my feet with a twenty-centimeter [eight-inch] fish attached. It was a shiny, silver horse mackerel.

The fish I had caught would certainly be my dinner that night, but the episode meant much more to me than that: my grasshopper strategy had been a success, and the fish had struggled with all its might, putting up a magnificent fight that awed and thrilled me. I had a lump in my throat. If only I could share the news with someone! But there was nobody around.

I yelled *"Banzai!"* to the mountains, and turned to the sea with my palms joined in a prayer of thanksgiving. Then I shouted, and sang, and jumped up and down for joy. The hills and the ocean had watched me and taken pity on me, and now they were holding out their hands to me.

From that day on, grasshopper-collecting and fishing became important parts of my daily routine. Sometimes— on stormy days when the waves were high—I had to go back to my tent empty-handed, but on the whole the sea was a bountiful and generous source of food. I ate horse mackerel grilled with salt, lightly roasted, in soups, in curry. Its flesh was firm, sweet, and delicious.

I spent two full days exploring the entire northern foot of Cerro Portezuelo, east to west, but the slopes only got steeper; I found no easy route to Selkirk's Lookout. Next I decided to follow the East River and the West River to their sources to see what I could find.

First, I tried the East River. It led me from valley to mountain ridge and back to valley again. When I left the grassy hillsides for the forest, I quickly found my way obstructed by fallen trees and tangled branches. I made my way deeper and deeper into the forest by stepping over the trees, crawling along them, or jumping; again and again I pushed through branch tunnels, heading higher all the time. As the climb got steeper I used my camera tripod as a walking stick, grabbed onto rocks with both hands, or held onto trees for support. It wasn't long before I was covered in sweat and breathing hard.

The forest was deeper on the steep upper slopes and was carpeted in ferns, probably because less sunlight reached the ground. Moss grew on stones and tree trunks. Everything I encountered could be useful for handholds and footholds, but just as often it made a formidable obstacle or barrier. Time and again, as I found my way cut off I would alter my route, searching for a slope that was easier to negotiate.

Finding tree roots as high as my waist, I would tap them with my tripod to test if they were solid; if all seemed well, I would set my weight on one and use it as a springboard to reach another. Often, however, to my frustration, the roots would turn out to be completely decayed: my feet would hit empty space, and pieces of the root and I would then tumble together to the bottom of the slope.

I was lucky I never hit my head. If I had, there would have been no one to come to my rescue. Sometimes as I was clawing my way tooth and nail up the slopes of Cerro Portezuelo, I would come to my senses for a moment and take a cool look at myself, clinging to tree roots and sweating blood. What the *hell* was I doing? It began to seem absurd—the very idea of crawling around on all fours like this on the side of a mountain on a tiny island in the middle of the South Pacific. To travel halfway around the world just so I could sail out on a sea of ordinary ferns, catch my foot in their twisted stems, and take a tumble was the height of folly.

I'd pause, bemused, while a flood of thoughts and feelings came and went inside me. Then in a moment of sober truth, I'd be forced to realize that I had no one with whom to share even such moments as these—and I would succumb to a wave of unbearable loneliness.

There was no relief from the wretched loneliness, either. All I could do was carry on mental debates with myself, or shout imprecations at the rocks and hills. They, of course, only listened in silence to my tirades.

In any case, grimly determined, I kept on clawing my way up the mountain in single-minded determination until I found it was hopeless: the slope turned into a cliff. I tried my best to find a way around it, but that too proved impossible. I would have to turn back.

The East River did not provide a route over the mountain.

On the way back, just as I was leaving the forest, I stumbled on a scattering of bleached bones in a pile of leaves. Judging from their size and thickness they were not human but belonged to a large animal such as a goat, cow, or horse. If they were goat bones, that could be an important clue, since I already knew that goat meat was a mainstay of Selkirk's diet on the island. Horses and cows came later, brought here by the Spaniards.

I examined each bone carefully, looking for signs of charring or marks from a knife or club. Then I scraped away leaves from the ground in a radius of two to three meters, finally coming upon a horned skull, leg bones, and giant ribs. Nowhere could I find any signs of human intervention.

Nowadays, herds of cows and horses inhabit the plains around Puerto Inglés. Looking at them from a distance, it was hard for me to judge whether they had gone wild or not, but the horns on the bulls were so long that it appeared they had not been trimmed in years. They took no notice of me as I went past them into the hills, but if I inadvertently took a step in their direction, one of the bulls—evidently the boss—would bristle and glare at me threateningly. What if he came at me and attacked me with those mean-looking horns? What would I do? The mere thought made me tense and weak at the knees.

Another time I found the body of a dead bull lying in a clump of grass, and I realized its bones were identical in size and shape to those I'd found near the East River— thus eliminating, unfortunately, the possibility that those bones had belonged to a herd of Selkirk's goats.

Next I set out to explore the West River. I headed southwest from the juncture of the two tributaries, and I was immediately struck by the rich growth of tall grasses. (In the southern hemisphere, the north side of a mountain is the sunny side, and vegetation grows better there than anywhere else.) I had high hopes that these tall grasses would provide me with a lead, because the descriptions of Selkirk's huts indicate that their walls were covered in long grasses. The type and exact length of the grasses are not known, but this was the first time I'd encountered waist-high grasses of any kind on the island.

Forging my way through the heavily bedewed grasses, I slowly climbed up the slope, my shoes and socks soaking wet. Now and then I came across furry little creatures that would quickly bound off through the grass. Like the horses and cows, those soft gray rabbits were descendants of animals brought over by the colonists; their dark eyes and erect little heads were an appealing sight, and I got a kick out of seeing them.

The sky had been cloudy when I set off, and before noon a moist wind began to blow, followed by drops of cold rain. I took shelter under a tree and waited for the rain to stop. Some birds fearlessly took shelter in the same tree as me, and I watched as raindrops ran down their beaks and wings and fell to the ground.

When the sky cleared, I resumed my walk and came across a tree where a whole flock of birds was perched. It was a maqui tree, which produces a sweet-sour berrylike fruit in summer. On my first day in San Juan Bautista I had noticed strange purple stains on the faces of some of the children, and one of the boys had told me that this fruit was the culprit—purple mouths and fingers were a traditional sign of summer on the island. As I munched away cheerfully and watched the dye do its work on my own skin, it occurred to me that this was a kind of initiation ceremony. Looking around, I saw there were a lot of the trees in the sunny lowlands: a secret orchard known only to the birds and me.

When I'd finished eating, I crossed over a hill, again becoming soaked with dew, and I entered the forest, which was no different from around the East River. There were lots of deciduous trees, their leaves fallen to the ground, their bare branches tangled in a labyrinth of arches, tunnels, and phantom caves. Then I saw something surprising: a lumber pile. Two stakes about six centimeters [about two and a half inches] across had been driven into the ground, holding several dozen pieces of wood all cut to the same size and keeping them from sliding downhill. Each piece of lumber, left there for God knows what purpose, was four or five centimeters [one and a half to two inches] across and about six meters [about twenty feet] long, with sharpened ends. Who had deposited all this wood in the middle of the forest, and why?

I used my tripod to scrape off dead leaves, looking for clues, but nothing came to light. The lumber was too narrow to be used as the foundation even for a lean-to, but I couldn't guess what other use it might have been put to. I decided to explore the surrounding area.

The sky was still overcast, and the ground was damp, the air moist. I went back down the hill and tramped back and forth, crisscrossing the area, but I found no open, flat land. The lumber made it likely that someone had once lived nearby, but if so, I was unable to find any trace of their presence.

Clearly, the lumber had not been there as long as the three centuries since Alexander Selkirk's day. The people living in Puerto Inglés must have cut it and piled it there for some reason.

In the end, I had no better luck with the West River than with the East. After climbing as high as I possibly could, I ran into another stone wall and was forced again to retrace my steps. There was no direct route to El Mirador from Cerro Portezuelo, then. The conclusion was inescapable, and I would have to adjust my thinking accordingly.

From the juncture of East River and West River, Cerro Agudo lay to the southwest and Cerro Alto to the northwest. Perhaps somewhere between those two peaks I might find a way through. Admittedly, that would be quite a roundabout way to Selkirk's lookout point. The plan did not seem very realistic, but if there was no direct route, I would have to consider a more circuitous path.

After several false starts, I set out across the foothills southwest of Cerro Alto. Unlike any other territory I had yet explored, this was barren, rocky ground. Where the going was steep I took a zigzag route, and where it evened out again I climbed straight up through breaks in the rocks. The hill was an upheaval of a submarine volcano, consisting of hardened lava from the long-ago birth of the island. Past about 200 meters [about 650 feet] above sea level, little by little low shrubs and grasses began to appear. The way seemed to lead straight toward a pass.

On the slopes of that hill, I stumbled on a metal fragment small enough to fit in the palm of my hand. Though badly rusted, it was a perfect rectangle with a small hole at either end. I was unable to find any other clues nearby, so its nature remained a mystery. I could only surmise that it might have been a nameplate or part of a gun. Metal objects corrode easily, but even so, judging from its condition it seemed very old.

Buoyed by the serendipitous discovery, I continued on my way until at last I stood on top of that nameless mountain. From there I could see that the western side of the island was mountainous and covered with dense ferns and grasses, nothing like the forests of Puerto Inglés. I went down the grassy slope on the other side of the mountain, trying to get as close to the sea as possible.

Thorny plants in the brush jabbed me, their sticky seeds attaching themselves to my shoelaces and trousers. The ground proved surprisingly crumbly, and I had to be extra careful or I would slide all the way to the bottom of the valley.

Little by little, the seaside cliffs drew nearer. Off in the distance I could see a tiny harbor known as Caleta La Va-

queria, where a dozen or more seals lay sunning themselves on rocks. That sight alone gave me a satisfying
thrill—but the harbor I was looking at lay in the opposite
direction from Selkirk's Lookout.

I'd already been on my own for eight days and so I only
had two days left to explore Puerto Inglés. Back at my
camp, to celebrate having finished one segment of the exploration of the island, I decided to take the day off. I
slung a hammock between two trees near the ocean and
lay down to let the soft breezes waft over me. I opened a
bottle of wine I'd left cooling in Robinson Crusoe's Cave
and spent the day sipping it and looking out on the sea
and sky, content to do nothing else.

The wine was a gift from George Simon, a Frenchman
who heard about me from the villagers and went to the
trouble of rowing over to see how I was doing. George
looked at me with curiosity and then handed me an arm-
load of wine and beer, saying it was his contribution to my
endeavor. Touched more than I could say that a total
stranger would do me such a kindness, I waved again and
again as I saw off his boat.

Now, as I lay dreaming in a pleasant state of intoxication, it struck me that the flow of time itself was different
on the island, its rhythm not the pulsing beat of seconds
and minutes but the slower beat of waves sweeping the
shore. Four times a minute. That worked out to 40 times
every ten minutes, 240 times every hour, 5760 times every
day. Day in and day out, the waves came and went at their
measured pace. Between sunrise and sunset, island time
was marked hazily by the sound of the waves.

In the afternoon I went for a walk on the beach and un-expectedly came across four dogs, a bitch and three pups. At the first sight of me they were on red alert and started howling. Was someone nearby, or were they strays? One of the mongrel puppies wagged its tail at me and came over to sniff me, head down. As I patted him on the head and back, the little fellow closed his eyes in bliss. His coat was soft, brown and fuzzy, with long white fur on the head and legs. His head was shaped kind of like that of a fox, but the eyes were round and dark. Even after his pals disap-peared he made no move to leave, and he sociably lay down beside me on the rock-strewn beach for an after-noon snooze.

We stayed that way for perhaps an hour. Then I began to feel too warm and decided to go back. The puppy trot-ted along after me, so I decided to invite him inside the cave. I set out a dish of water for him and gave him a lump of consommé, and he wagged his tail in pure pleasure. It delighted me to have found a little friend.

What should I call him? There could be only one choice: Friday. If Friday was going to hang around for a while, I reflected, from now on I'd have to catch enough fish for him, too. Just like that, my plain, lonely life was warmed and energized. After traveling to a tiny island on the remote side of the planet and living there in total iso-lation—even if only for three weeks—I had reached a conclusion: people aren't meant to live alone. My dog Fri-day made all the difference to my emotional state, turn-ing me around 180 degrees. My store of rice was getting low, but I didn't mind sharing it with him in the least. Peo-ple seem to live out their days caring only about them-selves, but in my state I discovered that having even a dog to care about makes life worthwhile.

But my time with Friday was all too brief. In no time at all, the other three puppies tracked his scent to my cave, and the four of them took off. Even so, I was full of gratitude. Brief as it was, the time shared with the puppy was a wonderful gift from Robinson Crusoe Island.

Clearly there was no route leading directly from Puerto Inglés to Selkirk's Lookout: the seaside way taken in by the dogs, as well as the way they ran off, on an animal trail leading to Cumberland, helped to convince me of that. The only way to get from Puerto Inglés to Selkirk's Lookout was the hard way, by hiking over the eastern ranges toward Cumberland and continuing on for several hours from there, in a tremendous expenditure of time and physical strength. But since Selkirk went daily to his lookout, that scenario was impossible. The facts neatly ruled it out.

I was satisfied; by climbing up and down and around these mountains myself, I had established that this part of the island could not have been where Selkirk lived.

Zone B: Villagra

When I got back to San Juan Bautista, the villagers had apparently forgotten all about me. Their gazes were aloof. I *had* gone the whole time without bathing or shaving, my skin was deeply sunburned and peeling, and the odor I gave off was probably too hideous for words. When I checked into my lodging and saw myself in the bathroom mirror for the first time in ten days, even I failed to recognize the wild man staring back.

I started right in on preparations for the next stage of my search, in Villagra, a hilly area on the southwest side of Selkirk's Lookout with a river flowing through its center. The area seemed promising not only because it was so near the lookout but also because it satisfied all my criteria for a living area.

Accounts by Selkirk's rescuer, Captain Woodes Rogers, contain frequent mention of "pimento trees": Selkirk built his huts with pimento wood, lit his fires with pimento chips, and seasoned his food with pimento fruit, known also as "Jamaican peppers." *Pimenta diocia,* or allspice, as the plant is commonly known, is a member of the myrtle family valued for its berries, which resemble in flavor a combination of cloves, nutmeg, and cinnamon. During the great age of exploration, they were highly sought after by mariners and traders dreaming of aromatic cargoes worth many times their weight in gold.

However, no book or document has ever clearly identified the trees found on the island in bygone centuries by Rogers and others. I had already spoken with Mauricio Calderon, director of Robinson Crusoe Island's branch of CONAF, whose opinion was firm.

"There are no allspice trees on the island," he insisted.

"Aren't there even any trees that are similar?" I pointed out to him again Captain Rogers's description.

"Rogers must have been talking about luma trees. It's the only tree on the island whose fruit can be used as a spice. There aren't very many of them left now, so the islanders hardly ever use the spice in cooking."

He gave me two luma leaves shaped like candle flames to help me to identify the tree in the forest.

Calderon also said that Villagra would have been an ideal choice for a place to live, with its luma forests, rivers, and flat, dry land—but that he strongly doubted I'd find Selkirk's huts were there. He based this conclusion on the difficulty of the route from Villagra to the lookout. The only path is so steep that it is all but impassable, and Calderon surmised that even Selkirk, a man of unusually robust health, would never have been able to make such a trip every day.

Several other points raised doubts in my own mind. First, Captain Rogers's *A Cruising Voyage round the World* contains the following entry for January 31, 1709: "At seven this morning we made the Island of *Juan Fernandez*; it bore WSW dist. about 7 Ls. [21 miles, 33.6 kilometers]." In other words, the day before his men went ashore and found Selkirk, Captain Rogers approached the island from the east-northeast, the opposite side from Villagra. In that case, Selkirk could *only* have spotted Rogers's ship from his eyrie in Selkirk's Lookout.

I found it hard to imagine that after more than four years of solitary exile, having made a shelter for himself and carved out a life, Selkirk would still have gone to the lookout every day and searched the horizon morning to night, watching breathlessly for possible rescue.

It also bothered me that no mention of Villagra occurs in records by later mariners and explorers, by that or any other name. Apparently, no one ever sought harbor or went ashore there for food and water. Contemporary U.S.-made maps reflect this singularity: anchor point in Villagra Bay is indicated at a depth of thirty meters [98.5 feet], but—unlike for Cumberland Bay and Puerto Inglés—there are no soundings for the shallows.

The luma forests, flat lands, and fertile valleys of Villagra provided excellent living conditions, but the harbor was difficult to access. Mentally I weighed the plusses and minuses, trying to calculate the probability that Selkirk had lived there, but I came up with no firm answer. To find out the truth, I would have to go see for myself.

My search would center this time on the long Villagra River, which winds down through the hills to the sea. Even my simple map showed this river plainly, along with the ravine it had carved out. I would focus on plains in the river vicinity, seeking out likely locales and narrowing them down by checking for the presence of luma trees and long grasses—and by relying on my own sixth sense.

But first, I would have to follow the river to its mouth to check on shoreline conditions. As I knew already from the map and from my own observations up in the Cessna 320, the island was ringed by steep cliffs with few points where ships could approach and drop anchor. Yet ease of access to the sea was a vital point in searching for Selkirk's huts, since he often went diving for fish and lobsters. I had to know whether or not the sea was in easy reach from Villagra.

Villagra is a sunken area southwest of Selkirk's Lookout, but its southeastern section contains the highest peak on the island, the forbidding Cerro El Yunque (915 meters [3000 feet]), while off to the north extends a range of towering peaks leading to Portezuelo. The river emerges from this mountainous interior, zigzagging down through valleys to the coast.

On the western side of the region is the strange sight of Cerro Tres Puntas stabbing the sky with three sharp peaks like saw blades. West of there, the ground becomes steadily more brittle, dry, and barren. Today there is a trail leading from Selkirk's Lookout to the westernmost point of the island, thus providing villagers access to the airport there.

Starting down the trail that led southwest from Selkirk's Lookout, I found it every bit as steep and tough to negotiate as Calderon had predicted. In many places it was less a trail than a series of footholds carved into precipitous rock walls. Moreover, the southern exposure meant that the area received little sun, so that well after a soaking rain the going remained wet and slippery.

In that moist environment grew giant butterburs (*Gunnera peltata*), rhubarblike herbs with big, long-stalked leaves that covered the narrow path entirely; I had to push my way through them to make any headway. The butterburs on Robinson Crusoe Island are among the biggest in the world, with leaves that often reach two meters [six and a half feet] or more in diameter. I found if I sliced through the thick stalk of one and held it in my hand, it made a fine, sturdy umbrella. I thought of the extreme difficulty with which the fictional Robinson Crusoe had fashioned an umbrella for himself. Selkirk would have had a far easier time since here umbrellas were everywhere, growing right in the ground.

Slipping and sliding, I made my way down toward the rolling hills of Villagra. The luma trees, muddy white in color, became a deep forest with ferns and moss underfoot. I felt transported back to ancient times. Finally I made my way to a low hill and pushed my way through the grasses growing on it toward the valley where the Villagra River ran. Probably because it was the dry season, this river, like the one I fished, was barely more than a slow trickle. Clusters of little butterburs grew in the riverbed, clinging to rocks here and there; many were withered for lack of water.

What surprised me most was the discovery that this wide hilly country consisted mostly of grassland. The edge of the forest receded along the mountainsides, and where the land was level, not a single tree grew. I was taken aback, having anticipated a lush, spreading forest.

I kept going, looking for the mouth of the river. Time and again I crossed to the other side, climbed a hill, made a circuitous detour, and climbed back down to the valley. As I got closer to the mouth of the river, the water moved faster and became frothier. The angle of descent grew steeper and steeper, until before I knew it I found myself clinging precariously to a sheer cliff face. Still, I wouldn't give up. Every inch of progress brought me nearer to my goal.

As I scrambled down the slope, the weather-beaten rocks crumbled away beneath my weight, unleashing a rain of debris. My hands were scratched and bleeding and I was sure that the fall would kill me. But my curiosity kept me going.

Finally I reached a point where I could see all the way along the coast. Was there any spot, however tiny, where one could safely reach the sea?

The river turned into a waterfall plunging straight over the edge of a bluff. Below was a maelstrom of angry waves, crashing against the rock with a roar and tossing up clouds of spray. The sight made me weak at the knees and dizzy, as if I myself were about to be swallowed in the boiling sea—yet there was my answer. There was no way anyone could live in Villagra and procure food directly from the sea.

I turned to go back and decided to enter the luma forest. Huge trees, their girth greater than my two arms could encircle, grew in clumps on the narrow slopes. The forest extended down into a deep valley.

As I walked on, the ground became moist, and in no time my shoes were covered with mud. I worked my way down into the valley, using the trunks, roots, and branches of the luma trees for support, and I found a surprise: the valley bottom was smooth, as if a road went through it. Big mossy stones lay all around. I continued for a while down this apparent road, where no grass grew and the bare ground lay exposed, until shortly I came on what seemed to be a man-made staircase leading up the mountainside, step after step.

For a moment, I felt as if I had stumbled on the remains of an ancient temple—but that couldn't be. I took a closer look at the ground and suddenly realized that all of the stones were perfectly round.

A river! That's what it was—the bed of an ancient, long-vanished river. "The country may fall, but mountains and rivers go on." So goes the old saying, but apparently it's not that simple. Mountains and rivers continually change in shape—some to be reborn, others to die. Standing on the remains of what was once another river, I felt the weight of the past. *And after all this time the island is still alive*, I thought, *still going strong.*

Climbing back up out of the valley, I saw brown, dried-up grasses waving in the wind from the ocean. Far ahead, cows roamed free on the hillsides, flicking their tails in bright sunshine.

Zone C: Cumberland

The last place remaining where I might discover traces of Alexander Selkirk's life on the island was Cumberland. Since this was where later colonists had naturally gravitated, there was a strong likelihood that Selkirk too had settled here; but even if he had, I could hardly expect to find his huts.

The Cumberland area boasts many attractive features, including plenty of flat land and a number of rivers. Development has slowly altered the land, however, so that it no longer looks the way it did three centuries ago. In and around the fishing village of San Juan Bautista by Cumberland Bay there now live some seven hundred islanders, and new houses are now going up even in the forest. As a result, my exploration faced certain natural limitations.

I had already asked many villagers if they knew anything about Selkirk's huts without getting the slightest lead. As at Puerto Inglés, it seemed entirely possible to me that colonists might have taken up where Selkirk left off, basing their lives here on the site of his former residence— and yet I could find no hint of any legend or oral tradition to corroborate the theory.

That left two possibilities. First, perhaps his huts lay deep in the forest, still undiscovered, unbeknownst to the villagers. Or perhaps he had lived somewhere inside the present village boundaries but the colonists had attached no special significance to his dwellings, and as time passed they had been forgotten or destroyed. If I was going to pinpoint where Selkirk lived, I would have to bank on the first alternative and penetrate deep into the forest where no one else went.

I began my exploration of the Cumberland forest in the vicinity of Selkirk's Lookout, choosing an area that had many rivers yet was seldom visited by islanders. Unfortunately, the day I set out I ran into a heavy rainstorm on the way. Suddenly the temperature plummeted, and large drops of rain fell out of an ash-gray sky. I sought shelter under a nearby tree, but the rain only came down harder, forcing me to get out my poncho and hunker down to wait out the storm.

I spent six hours watching rain fall off the tree leaves and run off in muddy streams on the ground, able to do nothing but stand there helplessly and wait it out.

Eventually evening set in, and it began to get dark. As soon as the rain let up a little, I left my backpack under the tree and dashed down the valley in search of a place to set up my tent. I finally found a likely spot: a cozy tunnel under the tangled branches of some tall blackberry bushes. It was a fine place to sit out the rain, but sharp thorns would make putting up the tent a challenge. The rain showed no sign of stopping, however, and I was not eager to get any wetter than I already was, so I gritted my teeth and put up the tent. When I got inside, I stripped off my wet things and stretched out flat on the ground, suddenly exhausted. I felt an attack of huge drowsiness, yet sleep was impossible: blackberry thorns poked through the material of the tent, sticking me everywhere in the arms and legs.

Even so, I managed to drift off. How long I may have slept I had no idea, but when I awoke it was pitch-dark. I lit a candle and looked at my watch: just past 8:30 P.M. A soft rain was still coming down.

I lit a small stove inside the tent and fixed some instant noodles I'd purchased in the village. As the tent filled with warm steam and the smell of consommé, I began to come back to life. I opened some canned clams and added them to the broth for a rich and satisfying evening meal.

The forests to the east of 565-meter[1850-foot]-high Selkirk's Lookout were deep, and the slope was steeper than I had expected. The days I spent wandering in those forests were a constant battle with blackberry thorns. I stuck to dry rivers and barely visible trails in hopes of making good headway, but the hard, sharp blackberry thorns held me back. I flailed at long brambles with my gloved hands and with sticks. They bounded back like cruel whips, scratching my face and snatching off my hat.

I decided to go down to the river, taking a roundabout route rather than plunging straight down through the Cumberland forest. The way I chose was fairly level but covered with a dense growth of blackberry bushes; in fact, I'd stumbled into a wicked den of thorns. With every movement I made, however slight, great thorns stabbed me on the head and face, arms and legs, piercing the thick cotton of my shirt and socks. Going forward was impossible, but backtracking was no easy task either. In any case, I was forced to abandon the idea of getting to the river by that route.

Apparently the only way to reach the river was to plunge straight down that steep slope. I started my descent, paying careful attention to my footing. Most of the trees were deciduous, so I had a good view of the bottom of the hill. But mixed in with the fallen leaves and the bare branches that I would reach out and grab to keep my balance were more of the thorny brambles, causing me to grit my teeth in pain once again.

Finally I began to hear the sound of the river. With water in plentiful supply, the blackberry bushes grew still bigger and taller, with longer brambles that twined together to form a dense, impenetrable wall of thorns.

Determined to get to the river, I made up my mind to search for the thinnest patch of blackberry bushes I could find, get down on all fours, and hack my way through at the roots. I wrapped a bandanna around my head, hat and all, and put on sunglasses. Since the ground was covered in fallen thorns, I held a big stone in each hand and pounded them into the dirt as I crawled along.

Despite all my efforts, I found no riverside spots where a person could set up house. All I found was a river skipping over stones. It was unrealistic to base my exploration of this area on rivers. I would have to change my strategy, look elsewhere for level ground.

I left the river behind and climbed back up another hill and down the other side until I came to a valley that had an old riverbed like the one in Villagra, flat and even, now and again forming something like stairs. Slowly I made my way up, but the forest was as dense as ever, moist and dark with almost no rays of sun penetrating the foliage. I would have to climb still higher.

As I went on, whenever I came to a likely looking place I investigated the area thoroughly, turning over stones and groping in thickets for clues. On and on through the forest I wandered, like a gold digger or someone possessed by a dream of buried treasure. But I unearthed no sign of any human presence.

The depths of the Cumberland forest, I found, consisted mostly of steep hills that fell away quickly; walking along the ridge was impossible. Down in the valleys the land was so damp and sunless that there seemed little point in exploring it for signs of human habitation.

The farther I went, the farther I seemed to get from any of the five necessary living conditions. I wandered around haphazardly, covered in sweat and mud, gritting my teeth—and yet the experience was by no means as bleak as it sounds. Once while I was fighting the blackberry brambles, to my intense delight I discovered a cherry tree, its branches heavy with luscious fruit. Just stuffing myself with all the cherries I could eat lifted my spirits and gave me consolation.

Here and there I saw eucalyptus trees, too. The leaves of the eucalyptus change shape as the tree grows, from round to sickle-shape, and just then they were changing colors as well. Yellow, orange, pink, gray, brown, wine-red: the ground was littered with sickle-shaped leaves of all hues, and the entire forest was at its gayest and most colorful.

Hummingbirds were another diversion. Some 350 varieties of the species are known to exist, mostly in Central and South America, but the ones I saw are unique to Robinson Crusoe Island. The birds that arrived there in the distant past gradually adapted to their new environment, evolving into a brand-new variety. The males are a vivid orange, the females a dull dark green, and both sexes proved to be full of curiosity. As I crashed noisily through the bushes, they came out of nowhere and hovered right in front of me, staring wonderingly at my every move. I tried greeting them with a cheery "Hey there, guys, what's up?" but they suddenly flew away in a whir of wings.

A hummingbird beats its wings 80 times per second, they say. Incredibly, then, for every minute of flying, it raises and lowers its wings 4,800 times. When I found the creatures sipping nectar from blackberry flowers, I stopped whatever I was doing and stood transfixed, watching them glide, dip, and hover. Defoe's *Robinson Crusoe* features Poll, a parrot that did much to amuse Robinson, and I couldn't help but think that these little fellows might have done the same for Selkirk.

As I wandered back and forth up hill and down dale without finding any clue or coming up with any new information at all, little by little I found myself working down the mountainside. I thought again of my five conditions: proximity to water and food supply; level ground; adequate sun; good access to the sea. Deep in the forest was plainly not the place to look for somewhere that would meet all those conditions. The closer I got to Cumberland Harbor, the more spots I found that easily filled the bill.

In one place outside the village, I had a sudden revelation. There were plenty of houses nearby, but that place itself was curiously untouched. Then in a sequestered recess I found a small white chapel standing quietly alone. The sight offered an excellent view of Cumberland Bay. What about a river? I looked around for one and found a dry waterway not far away. No water flowed in it anymore; grasses were beginning to take over the narrow riverbed, and small, bright orange flowers bloomed all around.

I went back to the chapel and began a detailed examination. No words were carved anywhere in the building to commemorate its founding or explain its origins to later generations. It was built on a still older stone foundation, most of which was now buried in grass and dirt. It seemed entirely possible that this might have been an old residence, a lookout place, or part of a building to house cannon.

In a clump of grass about a meter [three feet] to the left of the chapel I found a fifty-centimeter [twenty-inch] stick in the ground, for what purpose I could not tell. It did not seem terribly old, however, as the end had been carefully shaped with a plane of some kind. Another stick in the ground was longer by half and older as well, apparently on the verge of crumbling. There was a small amount of whitish bark still attached, enough to see that it came from a luma tree.

But why would there be a chapel in such a place? Too much time had elapsed for me to be able to find out anything concrete. The village elders only shook their heads, stumped. It was all a matter of conjecture.

Alexander Selkirk's huts, tangible traces of his life on the island, and all related clues had scattered and vanished in the intervening years; it was too late to arrive at the truth.

At the end of my three explorations, I made this surmise. While I had not come up with any material evidence to clinch my theory, this hill seemed the best place imaginable for the location of Selkirk's huts. Generations of later occupants had also found it a suitable living-place, as well as a perfect place for looking out on the ocean. The ruins left there gave ample testimony to settlements from different ages.

The first settlers, in fear of periodic raids by marauding pirates, might easily have wandered there in search of a place where they would be hidden from sight yet command a good view of the ocean. And, on finding what was left of the huts built there by Selkirk, they might well have begun to live there, attracted both by the livability of the site and its obvious strategic advantages. Then, as time went by and the need for a secluded place disappeared, people likely forgot about this place in the forest, remembering it if at all for the view.

I felt as if the tiny, isolated chapel built on an old stone foundation embodied long-ago prayers for safety on the sea and protection from predatory enemies, as well as profound respect for the first one ever to find this site and erect a shelter here.

CHAPTER

Five

The Lost Four Years
and Four Months

One day near the end of my stay on Robinson Crusoe Island, I slung a hammock between two pines in a grove overlooking the shore, lay back, and let my thoughts roam over the fifty-two months that Alexander Selkirk spent there in lonely exile nearly three centuries before. After a month of sleeping in a tent and trekking through trackless forests, I felt close to him in spirit. Having experienced feelings and moods that I imagined might have been similar to his, I could now, despite the many gaps in the record, glimpse what a tiny fraction of his four years' and four months' sojourn on the island must have been like.

Using accounts by Captain Woodes Rogers and others, fleshed out with my own suppositions, I will attempt below to recreate in my own words the firsthand experiences that became the inspiration for Defoe's *Robinson Crusoe.*

In September 1709, Scottish mariner Alexander Selkirk was deposited all alone on an uninhabited island in the South Pacific. Long after his ship had vanished from sight, even when the sun went down and it began to get dark, he kept his eyes trained on the horizon in the certainty that a white sail would soon appear. Of course they would come back for him. This had to be a passing whim of Captain Stradling. But please, dear God, let nothing like this ever happen to him again!

But his hopes came to nothing. Little by little, night set in. To the lonely and forsaken man, the slow onset of black night was unendurable. Weird, unfamiliar noises began to emerge from the forest after dark. Perhaps wild beasts, motionless during the day in shadows and caves, would come slinking out at night in search of prey. . . . Terror spurred his imagination, creating scenarios that tormented him and left him distraught.

Selkirk loaded his musket and held it at the ready. Every rustle added to his fears, ruling out any chance of sleep or rest. The night dragged on interminably. Even the starlight, which he was used to seeing on shipboard, had an eerie cast.

Next morning, he awoke to find himself leaning against a tree. His back ached from the awkward position he'd slept in, and his throat was dry and scratchy. He stuck his face in a nearby brook and drank his fill, emerging considerably refreshed—but only for the moment. The realization that he was truly alone soon plunged him back into deep gloom.

For the next few days he would go to a rock on shore and do nothing but sit and stare vacantly at the sea until nightfall brought on another abyss of despair. At first, his sorrow was so great that he had no appetite. Even after calming down a bit, he felt little inclination to eat until compelled by hunger, for a simple reason: he lacked both bread and salt.

Selkirk's only hope was that an English ship might come along and drop anchor in the harbor to replenish its water supply. No telling where the galley *Cinque Ports* was by now, he thought, though with greedy Captain Stradling at the helm, she was bound to be somewhere off the coast of Peru or Panama, chasing down enemy ships and seizing their rich cargoes. In that case, the galley would likely stop off here again on the way home.

What about Captain William Dampier and the *St. George*, from which the galley had long since parted company? They could show up at any time, too. Not only that, other privateer vessels could be on the way from England. Those waters were well known for the treasures waiting to be seized by any crew with their wits about them; however many ships set sail, there were always more sailors dreaming of quick riches than berths to accommodate them. Then again, English ships weren't the only ones likely to seek harbor here. If he ever fell into enemy hands, he'd be done for.

In the daytime, focused on the chance of a ship appearing over the horizon, he was buoyed with hope and anticipation; but at the end of the day when the inevitable disappointment set in he would collapse into a state of numb lethargy. Convinced then that no rescue was ever coming, he would look back on his past life and curse his stars. Full of resentment, he'd hurl foul-mouthed abuse at everything around him—the rocks and the trees, the sea and the sky. He even flung maledictions at the Creator himself. Lost in despair, he contemplated suicide, giving serious thought to the where and the how of it. Should he throw himself over a cliff? Hang himself? Or just point the muzzle of his musket at his throat and shoot?

Yet when he came to his senses in the dark of night, he knew that what he feared most of all was death itself. He didn't really want to die, not yet. Tomorrow a ship might come. Might as well wait one more day. . . .

Days he spent languishing at the seaside, nights he slept in the safety of a grove of trees. Always he told himself, "Today's the day," or "Tomorrow'll be the day."

When he left the galley *Cinque Ports* after a trifling altercation with Captain Stradling, Alexander Selkirk took with him a big wooden box containing all his belongings: clothes, bedding, a musket, gunpowder and bullets, tobacco, a hatchet, a knife, a kettle, a Bible, a few tools and other miscellaneous items, navigational instruments, and some books. That was all. In contrast, the fictional Crusoe had an enviable assortment of stuff, far greater in both number and kind. Where Crusoe was able to salvage from the wreck of his ship some sixty items, including a dog and a parrot, Selkirk had to make do with much less.

Handy as the musket was, his ammunition supply was finite. Shooting goats when they came to the brook for water was child's play, but once his bullets ran out, he'd have no way of obtaining food. Once he faced that stark fact, the gravity of the situation hit home. Nor was he enough of a marksman to bag his prey with a single shot.

At first, convinced that rescue was imminent, he couldn't bring himself to take his eyes off the horizon for a second, but as time passed, he was forced to acknowledge that he was starting to waste away. Day upon day of inactivity combined with little or no food had left him chronically fatigued. At this rate, he'd weaken steadily until he fell ill and died. Long sea voyages had taught him the hard way that food and exercise were the keys to life and health; he knew that shipmates who shut themselves up in their cabins soon lost appetite and fell prey to sicknesses that ultimately proved fatal. Leaving the shore involved the scary possibility that he might miss sight of a passing ship; even so, going inland in search of food began to seem more important. Surely he could find other lookout points. The thing was to get up, stretch and move around, and find something to eat. Besides, he had no clear picture of the layout of the island. In the end curiosity won out over fear, and he set out resolutely to explore the unknown interior. Doing so would bring him his first boon.

Selkirk followed the creek back across grassy hills and on into the woods, where he came across an amazing number of birds filling the forest canopy with joyous twittering and song. The birds' plumage was mostly an inconspicuous brown or gray, but they flitted adroitly from branch to branch and their voices soared high and pure, each with its own distinctive tone. As he walked through the forest, listening, Selkirk's taut nerves relaxed. He began to feel free and easy.

Far more goats than he had imagined inhabited the groves and plains; it was a veritable goat paradise. Nor was there any sign of dangerous wild animals, venomous snakes, or scorpions. In fact, as he examined the gentle hills, the trees, and the underbrush, he slowly understood that he was surrounded by a wealth of edible plants. Besides the succulent leaves of the cabbage tree, there were Sicilian radish, turnip, and watercress—all vegetables he'd eaten often back in Scotland.

He sat down by a babbling brook then and looked into its sparkling water, thinking of his far-away homeland. How was his father, he wondered. How many times had the old man warned him against becoming a sailor? The unheeded words fill his ears. If only he'd listened! This year he'd turn twenty-eight; had he stayed home, by now he'd be married, no doubt, with a family. But what was done was done. Impossible ever to go back and live one's life differently.

What about his mother, he wondered—did she still think of him? When he was little and came home in tears, she was always there to comfort him. Oh, if only he could go back now . . . back to hot soup, a soft bed, mother, home. How many days—or months—had he been in this godforsaken place, anyway? He had no idea. Maybe they'd all given him up for dead. Suddenly he yelled out at the top of his lungs, "Hey! I'm alive! I'm not dead, you hear me? I'm here! I'm right here!"

As night settled over the forest, Selkirk sobbed aloud. He had wept before, more times than he could count. It did no good, he knew, but thoughts of Scotland and his parents, brothers, and friends there brought on such fierce longing that he could not stop the tears from running down his cheeks.

Some small discovery would elate him, and the next instant he'd be sunk in misery again, tortured by thoughts of home. Happiness existed side by side with heartbreak.

Later, when he went back to the shore to look for food, he found it taken over by huge, ferocious seals. The animals were a damned nuisance. Their tough, rubbery meat was inedible, and their presence made foraging in the water risky. The minute he came near one of them it would turn with an ungodly roar and attack, ready to take a bite out of him.

Finding a spot a safe distance from the seals, he strode into the water. Using a harpoon that he'd fashioned himself, he was able to catch all he wanted of shellfish, great big lobsters and sea turtles, while all kinds of fish swam right up to him without fear. When he scaled the rocky cliffs, he found countless petrel nests containing a ready supply of fresh eggs that was his for the taking.

Everywhere he looked, Selkirk found plenty to eat— and when he learned to start a fire, he was able to improve the flavor of goat meat and lobster by boiling or broiling it. Having seen sailors briskly rub two sticks together to start a fire, he tried it with various kinds of wood, so intent on learning that he rubbed his palms raw. By the time he began to work up a sweat, a thin wisp of smoke finally went up and red sparks flew, igniting dry leaves.

Luma wood worked the best, he found. The luma trees also produced fruit much like Jamaican peppers, or allspice, which he used dry and crushed to reduce the gaminess of meat and bring out the flavor of vegetables.

Thus aided by his environment, Selkirk was able to divert his mind somewhat, but melancholia and the inconsolable sorrow of remaining entirely alone in that godforsaken place with no chance of rescue took a steady toll, plunging him steadily into a pit of hopelessness.

One day as he was chasing a goat, he came unexpectedly on a pleasant piece of rising ground that formed a small, natural lookout high atop the cliffs, revealing both the eastern and western sides of the island to his view. For Selkirk, it was a heaven-sent place to keep watch over the sea. As long as he stood there, any ship approaching the island would be clearly visible. From then on, Selkirk made a point of visiting the lookout daily—although until he got the knack of it, scrambling up the steep, fern-covered hillsides was difficult.

When it became clear that a quick rescue was not in the cards, Selkirk began to consider ways to make his existence on the island more comfortable. Around the onset of the rainy season, mornings and evenings were chilly, and he needed to do more than huddle in a pile of fallen leaves if he was ever to get a good night's sleep. Rain fell all day, soaking everything and making dry wood all but impossible to find, and at night the cold was intense. Sometimes he fell ill and couldn't get up for days. All of this made the need for some sort of housing imperative.

By now he'd been all over the island (which was so small that if not for the steep range of mountains bisecting it, he could have walked it from end to end in a couple of days) and had several likely spots in mind. He gave the matter a lot of thought. First, wherever he chose to live would have to be near a good supply of fresh water. There were dozens of streams, but few that wouldn't turn to a trickle in the dry season. Next, his living area would have to be on level ground, of course, in a nice sunny spot near the lookout, which he visited every day. And finally, it should command a clear view of the ocean.

Overcoming the difficulties of building a house was a considerable challenge for Selkirk. Cutting down a luma tree was a backbreaking undertaking, to start with. Selecting timber of various dimensions and storing it in one place was a hard job for one man—he'd never dreamed that a log could weigh so much. His back was soon killing him. In all his life, he'd never built a house before, and he regretted not having paid more attention to the process back in Scotland. The frame he put up by trial and error was off kilter and had a habit of collapsing suddenly, never actually hurting him but providing many a harrowing experience. Every time that happened he was ready to call it quits, but when night rolled around and he lay shivering again, he knew in his bones that he really had no choice.

The more mistakes he made, the more he began to get a feel for the work, until he could see clearly what was wrong and how to improve it. When his efforts were rewarded and the frame finished, he made outer walls by layering long grasses to guard against wind and rain, while on the inner walls and the floor, he spread goatskins to keep out the cold.

Finally his hut was finished.

Knowing that he had built a solid hut all by himself gave Selkirk unshakable self-confidence and taught him that life on the island was not all bad. Concentrating on a project had allowed him to forget his wretched loneliness for a while, if not wipe it out completely. When he came out of his shell and acted on his environment, nature responded with limitless beneficence and wisdom.

Just as it was for Robinson Crusoe, the Bible was a spiritual anchor for Selkirk. Back in Scotland and during his life at sea, Selkirk had not been a particularly zealous Christian. Religion, with its prayers for safety and happiness and its teaching that salvation depended not on one's own efforts but on the grace of God, had always been anathema to his forceful, independent personality. It offended his notion of the ideal life.

His father was a good example of the kind of man Selkirk had never wanted to be, leading a life of pious prayer and quiet discipline. Rebellion had led him straight to the sea, where he had promptly put all thoughts of God out of his head. Yet now, God alone could save him.

Selkirk began setting aside a portion of each day for reflection and thanksgiving. What would have become of him had there been wild animals on the island? Even with his musket for self-defense, he would have been killed and eaten long ago. God had seen fit to populate the island not with savage beasts but with countless goats whose flesh he ate and whose soft skins kept him warm. The more he thought about it, the more clearly he saw that everything he had accomplished, from learning to start a fire to building a hut, was done not alone but with divine mercy and help. True, he had carved out a life with his own strong life-force and patience, indomitable spirit, and creative resourcefulness, but above all else it was the abundance of life on the island that had made it possible. He sensed God's hand over him, keeping him alive, and he was profoundly grateful.

Just when life began to settle into a comfortable pattern, his living area became infested with rats. Transported to the island via pirate ships and merchant vessels, the pesky creatures had quickly multiplied until they were everywhere. Big, bold rats would pad noisily around his hut while he slept, gnawing on the walls and central support; what was worse, they brazenly sunk their long, sharp teeth in his clothes, arms, and legs, even his face.

Finally, Selkirk set out to do something about it. He decided he would tame some of the cats that had gone wild after being abandoned on the island by their owners. He quickly won them over with goat meat; soon they would gather by his hut whenever they were hungry, coming and going in perfect freedom, showing up again just when he thought they'd gone away for good. Something in their capriciousness reminded him humorously of himself, and he grew tremendously fond of them.

When a female cat gave birth one day to a litter of kittens and presented them to him, Selkirk was as overjoyed as if they were his own flesh and blood. As they grew he spent hours watching the little things walk around with their tails in the air. The cat family served to keep his hut and its environs rat-free, but more than that, he loved them for themselves, treating them like friends and family. He entertained the kittens with Scottish airs and sea chanties, dancing with cats and young goats that he tamed, to while away the hours.

Such diversions notwithstanding, life fell into a predictable routine. He spent the better part of each day perched in his lookout and, apart from working at some project or other, the rest of the time he read his Bible—at least once a day—until his mind grew tired. His supply of musket powder by now low, he never fired a shot anymore unless it was absolutely necessary. The edible fruits and vegetables he found on his walks changed with the seasons; what he liked best of all was the sweet pulp of the coconut. The fruit of the luma trees he harvested carefully once a year, setting it out to dry in the sun so that he could use it as a spice year round. The more time passed, the more comfortable he felt with the rhythm of island life, and the better he adapted to it.

One day as he was standing as usual at his lookout, he realized a ship was about to drop anchor in the harbor. Exultant, he tore down the hillside in a flash, making straight for the beach where the men would be coming ashore. But when he got a good look at the ship, he was forced to turn around and flee noiselessly away. It was a Spanish vessel. If Spanish sailors caught him, they would either kill him on the spot or cart him off to spend the rest of his life slaving in a mine. Several of the Spaniards caught sight of him as he fled and fired potshots in his direction. They took off after him, but he knew the island like the palm of his hand and soon left them behind.

In their excitement, the Spaniards fired again at random—barely missing Selkirk's head. He cried out in surprise, and the chase was on again. Selkirk ran blindly through the forest and then scrambled for dear life into the crotch of a tall tree. He clung motionless, scarcely breathing, as the Spaniards came and milled around at the foot of the tree, casually relieving themselves under his nose. In the end, unable to find him, they shot several goats and went back to shore.

The Spanish galley stayed moored at the island for several days. Every time the crew fired a thunderous volley of shots, the island creatures would cower in terror, and Selkirk too laid low, crouching in shadows and keeping close watch on the visitors' movements. He couldn't help noticing the change in himself. In the beginning, he had craved any kind of human contact, but now that these ruffians were here in front of him, he wanted nothing better than to see them go. It went beyond any question of national loyalty. He perceived these men, the first he'd seen in a long time, as intruders who threatened his way of life.

For years now, Selkirk had lived close to the island creatures, sharing with them his joys and his woes. When it rained they all got a soaking, and when the rays of the sun were warm and inviting, they basked in them together. He had come to understand and sympathize with the creatures, and seeing them tremble now in fear at men's willful behavior caused him much distress.

After that episode, Selkirk stopped wishing so strongly for a ship to come in. He never lost his desire to return home to Scotland, but he hated the thought of strangers coming to trample the island. His feelings were torn.

Eventually, he built a second hut at a little distance from the first, out of sight of potential invaders. He took care to avoid walking the same way every day, so as not to beat paths in the ground. Wary after his near-calamitous encounter with the Spaniards, he now made sure that his house and his life blended in seamlessly and invisibly with the life of the island.

He used the smaller of the two huts mainly for cooking and eating, the other for sleeping and devotions. Building the second hut wore out his hatchet and the blade of his knife. Once as he was walking along the shore, he came across some barrel hoops left behind by the Spaniards. He flattened them with stones, ground them thin and attached wooden handles, making a set of fine new knives. Selkirk did not rely solely on tools for his living, however. Years of ripping goat flesh and breaking lobster shells with his bare hands had thickened and toughened his skin so that his hands themselves functioned as a good set of tools.

Eventually, his clothes wore out. Using goatskins and strips of leather, he fashioned new clothes for himself, including a cap, coat, and trousers. He sewed pieces of linen together, using worsted yarn from his old socks, and made a rough shirt. In all his sewing, he used a nail as needle.

As time went by and Selkirk adapted more and more to his environment, he watched the supplies he'd brought with him dwindle or cease to be useful. The loss of his cherished gunpowder and bullets was the most distressing. He tried building a stockade to herd goats in, but that plan did not succeed very well. Then he came up with another idea: he would try to catch goats by running after them.

At first it didn't go at all well, and he wound up racing up and down the slopes at random, but in time he got the hang of it. His encyclopedic knowledge of the island terrain served him well. He would run zigzag up a slope and drive a goat toward the edge of a cliff, forcing it over the edge. In time, he was swift enough to catch the goat alive at the top of the cliff before it took the plunge.

Selkirk kept an account of each goat he killed, and the tally soon reached five hundred. He caught as many more, releasing them unharmed with only an identifying mark on the ear. This fact, recorded in Captain Woodes Rogers's account, was verified in 1741 when George Anson visited the island and discovered goats with marks on the ear, thus vouching for Selkirk's credibility. No trace was ever found, however, of the trees on which he supposedly carved his name and marked off the passing days.

There were always hardships to be overcome. No sooner was one problem solved than the next reared its head. He finally acquired the nimbleness to chase after goats and catch them alive with his bare hands—only for his shoes to wear out. He developed blood blisters on his feet and when they burst, stepping on even a small pebble set off shock waves of pain. Still, he was desperate to secure food. In the end, walking and running about shoeless made his feet as hard as granite, enabling him to fly through the woods with greater freedom and swiftness than ever. Captain Rogers mentions that Selkirk was barefoot when found and that although he was given a pair of shoes, he was unable to wear them because they made his feet swell.

One day Selkirk chased a goat to the brink of a precipice and fell with it over the edge into a ravine more than 100 meters [328 feet] below. Rain had softened the ground and he misread the goat's movements, and the next thing he knew he was tumbling through air all the way to the bottom. He bruised himself badly and hit his head hard, losing consciousness. He lay there for hours, knocked out cold. When he came to he felt sick, and his joints were so stiff and painful that movement was laborious. He was thirsty, but there was no water nearby. He continued to lie there in a swoon all night. In the morning, he became aware of something soft and pleasant against his skin, and he realized as he came to his senses that he was lying sprawled on the body of the dead goat.

He had barely escaped with his life. Only because the goat fell along with him and landed under him had he survived, the goat dying instantly. Selkirk trembled at the narrowness of his escape, patting the goat's body over and over.

For the next two days he was scarcely able to move, but he managed somehow to crawl the kilometer and a half [about a mile] to his hut. It was another ten days before he was able to get up and move around again as freely as before.

This incident impressed upon him strongly that the circumstances he found himself in were not owing to mere chance or coincidence. He became convinced that the moment he fell over the precipice, some huge power had come into play, saving him, and that he owed his life to divine providence. He never lost that faith; always, even when he later came down with fever or dysentery, he clung to it for support.

Four years of continued isolation went by. By then, Selkirk had no qualms about living out the remainder of his life on the island. He was the only human around, but he had plenty of animal company. Not only that, the island was clearly his possession, his kingdom, and he the undisputed lord and king. His parents and friends back home must have long since given him up for dead, and indeed he had gone through something much like a death and rebirth. His father, he found, had been right after all: the way to happiness was to live each day soberly and honestly, step by step. His new way of living was orderly and temperate, and filled with thanksgiving.

His mother had been right, too, though, in saying that a man should pit himself against some challenge and seek victory. Loneliness, terror, melancholy, hardship: day by day he had confronted these head-on, and he had come out victorious.

Of course he would still like to go home, if such a thing were possible. But even if he ended his days here, he could say that, all in all, his life had been good. He reckoned that he owed his ability to survive on this uninhabited island to three things: humble thanks to divine providence, a spirit of philosophical acceptance, and presence of mind.

February 1, 1709. On that day, four years and four months after he began his lonely existence on the island, Selkirk spotted a tiny white sail on the horizon. What was this, more Spaniards? He heaved a sigh and prayed that the ship would sail past without stopping. Far better to stay here his whole life than to end up in *their* hands. He climbed up to his lookout and watched the ship pull near, slowly making out that there were not one but two. Dusk was approaching by the time he made out the Union Jack fluttering on each ship's prow. They were English ships! He could go home!

Brilliant light filled his heart. Was this a dream?

Night's curtain was falling, but Selkirk ran madly down the mountainside and into the woods, gathered up armfuls of dead leaves and fallen branches, and piled them high on the beach.

After dark the two ships were each hung with lanterns, tiny lights bobbing in the gloom. On shore, Selkirk rubbed two sticks of luma wood furiously together, producing sparks that gradually became a huge bonfire. The flames were fanned by the wind, bits and pieces of the fire scattering and dying out deep within the forest. Whole flocks of birds rose up and wheeled off in surprise with a sudden whir of wings.

The huge red fire lit up the surroundings, and billows of smoke rose into the sky like an enormous gray cumulus cloud. But would the people on board see the light of the fire? Watching the wavering light of the lanterns, Selkirk grew uneasy. *Send me a signal if you see it,* he thought. *Why don't you make some response? I'm here! I've waited so long . . .*

Selkirk kept the fire going all night without sleeping, continuing to signal the English vessels as best he could. When morning finally dawned, bringing improved visibility, he could watch the ships draw closer to the harbor. Finally a small boat was let down and headed straight for shore. Selkirk ran for the place where it would land. This was it, his moment of rescue. God, how he had waited for this! Wordless prayer filled his mind and thoughts.

When the eight men in the boat set foot on shore, Selkirk ran toward them in a transport of joy. Huge tears spilled from his eyes.

When I returned to the fishing village of San Juan Bautista, I visited the barracks of the Chilean national forestry agency (Corporation National Forestal, or CONAF). It was a Sunday, so the office was closed. I rang the doorbell at Mauricio Calderon's home, and his wife came to the door. He was away on a field survey, she informed me, and would not be back until around six that evening.

I went back to the village and sat on a bench, looking absently out to sea. Before I knew it, I was surrounded by passers-by who stopped to chat about all sorts of things. A construction worker pointed to a huge tanker that had just anchored in the port. "It takes forever to get anything built in this place," he lamented. "See that? Even foundation stones have to be brought all the way from South America, load after load." He apparently was not an islander.

A young fellow who'd been yelling "Hello? Hello?" into a public telephone had this to say, mixed with a sigh: "Service is probably bad on the continent, but here it's impossible. The wires are jammed." Telephone service had just been installed, and people were so excited about it that communications were affected.

A fisherman's son told me his dream. "I wish I had a motorcycle. I'd like to race a horse down Main Street. Which do you think would win?" He had no idea which one was faster, a horse or a motorcycle. Someday, after he grew up, he would undoubtedly have a chance to find out. It wouldn't be much longer, either.

Three hundred years after Selkirk had lived here, the island had undergone significant changes. Though still a quiet place, San Juan Bautista was definitely being lapped by the waves of civilization. Ships that were the bearers of civilization formed the heart, the very life's blood, of the community.

At noon, I decided to pay a call on old Monsieur Simon, the Frenchman who'd kindly brought me wine at Puerto

Inglés. He was a retired military man over sixty years old who now owned a house on the island. In his youth he'd been a soldier, serving in a crack parachute corps in Indonesia and Algiers and later as a commando in the Foreign Legion. His eyes were piercing and the muscles of his arms and legs looked as sturdy as ever. His right index finger and middle finger were missing, but when I asked what had happened, he only answered laconically, "Trouble." He had no hair on his head, and he seemed at first utterly unapproachable; but when he caught sight of me his face softened.

Monsieur Simon spent summers in France and came here every year for the winter, enjoying a leisurely and relaxed old age. Visiting his house was for me like returning to the countryside. He plied me with more wine and beer than I could drink and even made space for me to spend the night, providing me with everything I could want. It turned out that he sympathized greatly with my mission, having once set off alone for Puerto Inglés and lived in Robinson Crusoe's Cave just as I had. Just as my time on the island was the fulfillment of a boyhood dream, for Simon the island represented the final paradise of his old age.

When I stepped inside his house he was standing in the kitchen, drawn to his full height, wearing a bright T-shirt. He greeted me jovially, asked where I'd been keeping myself, and insisted I stay to lunch.

Our meal was a noisy affair. Simon had an old tape deck on which he played first the Marseillaise, then various war songs, all at top decibel. That was because he was hard of hearing—but to me it felt uncomfortably like having to eat in the military with my back ramrod straight. Sometimes he would stick in explanations—

"These are the trumpets of the alpine corps," or "This is the song of the Foreign Legion"—while waving his hands expressively. He made the same explanations again and again.

After beer, wine, and chicken livers, I didn't know how to thank him, but there was more: next came dessert, then coffee.

By now it was past six, the hour when Mauricio Calderon would be returning home. As I excused myself, Simon told me he would be having rabbit that evening, and he urged me to come back for dinner.

I was due to leave the island in two days, and there were a number of issues I wanted to discuss with Mr. Calderon that evening. I wanted to share with him all that I had seen and felt on the island, and I had a few lingering questions that I hoped he could clear up. When I arrived at his house at six-thirty, he was there. His little daughter, a sweet thing of five or six, served me an ice-cold Coke that I sipped as we talked.

"You know," I said, "I took a good look at Robinson Crusoe's Cave, and frankly it strikes me as impossible that Selkirk could have lived there. Yet I couldn't help noticing that CONAF has a sign up saying that he did."

He smiled ruefully. "Much as I hate to admit it, there's not one iota of evidence supporting the theory that he ever lived there. After people settled the island, that story about the cave just came out of nowhere. It's only that it looks so much like the cave described in the novel. As a matter of fact, there are a lot of gaps in our knowledge of the island's history. We really can't explain those cannons lying around on the shore, either, or the foundations of the stone houses. Anyway, until we do find evidence of where Selkirk lived, I don't know what harm it does to leave the sign up. It's stimulating to the imagination."

I brought up another topic. "You know, I walked over nearly the entire island, and I never saw a single goat." I showed him the list I had compiled of island plants and animals mentioned in the literature on Selkirk.

"There are two hundred goats on the island now. We've finally reduced it to that number."

"You're trying to get rid of them?"

"That's right. When CONAF was established, our first assignment was to eradicate the island of goats. They were ripping up rare vegetation indigenous to the island and devouring it. Nowadays they only live on mountains 400 meters [about 1300 feet] over sea level or higher."

"I did see lots of cows, horses, and rabbits."

"Those were all introduced to the island well after Selkirk's day. The cows are a big headache. Ten years ago they caused no end of trouble between the forest rangers and the villagers."

"Why is that?"

"The law says there can only be 130 head of cattle, and anyone bringing livestock into the national park will be fined. The cows represent another threat to native vegetation, but at the same time they are indispensable to the villagers. That's the source of the friction. Right now there are 175 head on the island, well over the limit. In Puerto Inglés alone there are 50. It's completely illegal."

"Who's breaking the law?"

"The owners of the cows are the wealthiest families in the village, and the village headman and the police have no choice but to look the other way . . . this is a peaceful place, but where people's interests are involved, the existence of a single cow takes on extra meaning." Mauricio

Calderon looked down at the list of plants and animals I'd handed him, his face a mix of emotions.

Most of the wild cats that once populated the island had been exterminated by CONAF. Thanks to reckless hunting, the seal population had shrunk from several tens of thousands to 2,500, and the cabbage trees and chonta palms were in danger of extinction because of damage inflicted by humans. The list I had made to aid me in finding Selkirk's lost huts turned out to be a handy checklist of disappearing life forms.

"When people came here to live, the first thing they did was burn the fields to clear them and make pastures to support their livestock. Whole forests were burned down and replaced with pines and eucalyptus."

I was astonished. "Are you telling me that neither pines nor eucalyptus are native to the island?"

"That's right. People planted them because they were useful for building houses and boats and lobster traps. Maqui and blackberry bushes from the continent are another threat to indigenous vegetation."

I couldn't believe my ears. So even they were interlopers?

"Yes," Mr. Calderon confirmed. "Unfortunately, birds are fond of sweet berries, and they spread seeds of the introduced species all over the island in their droppings."

Presently the island hosts 362 plant species, of which 101, or fewer than one-third, are indigenous. Roughly half of those species—45 in all—are endangered, and fragrant sandalwood is already extinct.

Having come this long way in an attempt to fill in a gap of three hundred years, I'd wound up face to face with the present reality of nature being driven into a corner. On this island, seemingly so remote and isolated from civilization, I had encountered a paradigmatic example of modern environmental ills. Carl Skottsberg, the Swedish botanist who visited Robinson Crusoe Island in 1908 in search of new plant species, returned in 1917 and went on to achieve fame for ecological studies he carried out there with immense curiosity and patience. He was also the first to grieve over the severity of environmental destruction on the island and sound a warning for the future. He left several suggestions for future generations in order to protect the island's unique natural environment, the property not of any one country but of the world. "These," he wrote, "are the rules:"

> *to limit plantations and fields to the waste-land on the north side of Masatierra;*
>
> *to encourage gardening for local consumption;*
>
> *to declare war on the introduced noxious weeds, goats, and rabbits;*
>
> *greatly to reduce the number of domestic animals and to keep them out of the native forest;*
>
> *to reduce the number of wild goats on Masafuera[1] and keep it to a minimum or, which would be the best, to exterminate them;*
>
> *to teach the inhabitants not to disturb Nature's equilibrium;*
>
> *to enforce the Law of Jan. 31, 1935, by appointing a sufficient number of salaried supervisors and guardians.*[2]

---

1. Author's note: Second of the islands in the cluster 144 kilometers [about 90 miles] west of Robinson Crusoe Island; its name today is Alexander Selkirk Island.

2. Quoted in Ralph Lee Woodward, Jr., *Robinson Crusoe's Island: A History of the Juan Fernández Islands* (Chapel Hill: University of North Carolina Press, 1969), pp. 228–29.

Sunrise at Largo Bay, Scotland

Lower Largo

Main Street of Lower Largo

Selkirk's birthplace

Rape blooms in Largo in May

The statue in Selkirk's hometown of Largo, Fife, Scotland

Cessna 320 to Robinson Crusoe Island

Mules are still in use at San Juan Bautista

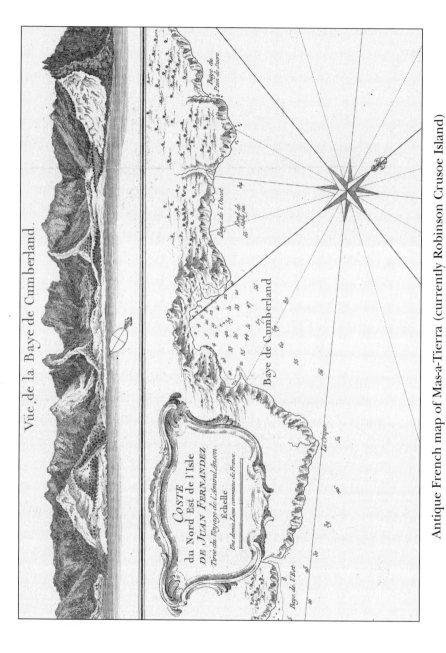

Vüe de la Baye de Cumberland.

COSTE
du Nord Est de l'Isle
DE JUAN FERNANDEZ
Tirée du Voyage de l'Amiral Anson.
Echelle
Une demie Lieüe commune de France

Baye de Cumberland

Baye de l'Est

Baye de l'Ouest

Baye du
Puits de Barre

Antique French map of Mas-a-Tierra (currently Robinson Crusoe Island)

A monument by Commodore Powell of HMS *Topaze,* currently the sole tangible reminder of Selkirk's presence on Robinson Crusoe Island

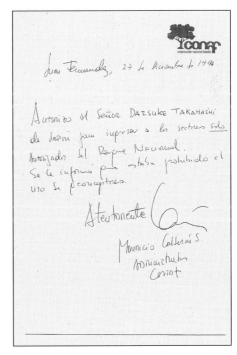

Permission issued by CONAF for my exploration on the island

View from Selkirk's Lookout

Robinson Crusoe's Cave

Ruin of human habitation at Puerto Inglés

View from a hill in Puerto Inglés

Whitened bones of a cow in Puerto Inglés

Drinking water on a hill in Puerto Inglés

Lunch at Robinson Crusoe's Cave

A feast at Puerto Inglés

In Villagra

Finally I reached the top
of the cliff in Villagra

Wandering in the bush of Cumberland

December 13, 1721 excerpt from the log of the HMS *Weymouth*, with nota-
tion of Selkirk's death. *(Crown copyright material in the Public Record Office,
London, is reproduced by permission of the Controller of Her Britannic Majesty's
Stationery Office.)*

To His Grace the Duke of Hamilton &c:

The most Humble Petition of —
                                    Frances Selkirk

Most Humbly Sheweth.

That Yr Graces Petitionr is the Widdow of Alexander Selkirk who was left on the Desolate Island called Ferdinando where he continued alone Four Years & Four Months all which time he kept a Journal of his Observations as also of the Voiages he made with the Capt: Dampiere as also in the Duke which Took the Aquapulca Ship in the South Sea which Ship Yr Petitionrs Husband had in the Charge as Comander to Bring to England And upon his Arrival His late Grace Yr Most Noble Father then Desireing to see the Abovesaid Journall Yr Petitionr: said Husband Did Leave it with him after which proceeding again to Sea on another Voiage Dyed in the same And Yr Graces Petitionr: being now Reduced to very low circumstances is Advised that said Journall would be of some considerable Advantage to her in her Present circumstances And Most humbly hopeing that it may have bin Reserved safe in the Library of Yr Most Noble Predecessor. ——

Therefore Yr Petitionr: most Humbly Begs That your Grace in Yr Great Goodness would be pleased to condescend to give such directions as thereby Your Petitionr: may have the said Journall Delivered to her. ——

And Yr Petitionr: as in Duty Bound for Yr Grace Shall ever Pray &c

A letter sent by Selkirk's widow, Frances, to Duke Hamilton requesting the return of her late husband's diary (© *Lennoxlove House*)

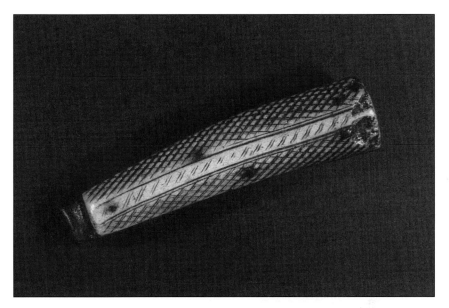

Alexander Selkirk's knife handle *(© Fife Council Museums East)*

Alexander Selkirk's sea chest *(© 1999 The Trustees of the National Museums of Scotland)*

Coconut cup that belonged to Alexander Selkirk *(© 1999 The Trustees of the National Museums of Scotland)*

Remnants of what may have been Alexander Selkirk's shelter, shown to me by a resident of the island during my second trip to Robinson Crusoe Island

Skottsberg's approach was thoroughgoing, his call for the extermination of all goats on the island provocative. Brought there originally by humans, years later they were branded as pests by humans and made the object of an extermination campaign. Don't goats have a right to life?

When environmental protection conflicts with animals' right to life, humans are forced to make an ultimate choice. Sadly, animals are indeed being hunted down and killed today in order to protect the environment.

In January 1966, as a ploy to boost tourism, the Chilean government rechristened the island "Isla Robinson Crusoe" [Robinson Crusoe Island]. But as one might guess from the harshness of its terrain, the island is not well suited for tourism (unlike the more famous Easter Island, also Chilean territory, which attracts visitors from around the world). From the standpoint of conservation, the island's unpopularity has been its salvation. CONAF has taken Skottsberg's admonitions to heart and is in the process of administering them. The yearly budget for the program is seven thousand dollars, most of which goes for patrol boat fuel, upkeep for the island's three lookout posts, construction, and personnel expenses for rangers.

Calderon spoke quietly of his personal dream. "On top of the highest peak on the island, Cerro El Yunque, is a plant that grows nowhere else on earth, called yunquea. Unfortunately, it has decreased sharply in number, and today there are only twenty samples surviving. One of these days I intend to climb up those 900-meter [about 3000-foot] cliffs and retrieve some seeds. We could germinate them here at CONAF, grow them, and take them back up to the top of El Yunque. I don't know if it will happen in my lifetime, but at least by the next generation, yunquea flowers will bloom again all over the mountaintop."

To make flowers bloom on a mountaintop where scarcely any human sets foot: what a fine dream, I thought.

My investigation into the vestiges of Alexander Selkirk's life on this island was now over. Apart from the forest depths, the island I had seen differed vastly from what it was in Selkirk's day, extensive ecological change having caused many species of vegetation to become endangered or extinct. The age had changed, and the environment with it. If all trace of Selkirk's huts had been destroyed in the process, that was, although regrettable, both natural and inevitable. But I had learned something of far greater importance: Alexander Selkirk, the model for Robinson Crusoe, was an ordinary fellow.

What I would like to call attention to, more than Selkirk's legendary (and exaggerated) resourcefulness, is the island's own richness. Neither harsh desert nor freezing tundra, the beautiful terrain is bursting with life. Nature there rewards human ingenuity with unstinting generosity. That is why Selkirk flourished on the island, and that is why his true adventures later formed the basis for Daniel Defoe's immortal literary classic.

Robinson Crusoe—28 years, 2 months and 19 days

Alexander Selkirk—4 years and 4 months

Daisuke Takahashi—1 month

The time I spent in nature on Robinson Crusoe Island was pitifully short, but I remain filled with gratitude, knowing it was the island itself that blessed me and made my stay comfortable. Still, environmental degradation is taking its toll. I can only pray that the legendary island that gave birth to Robinson Crusoe may yet stay unchanged for ages to come—so that the dreams of future children may not be spoiled.

CHAPTER

Six

Vanished at Sea

On January 7, 1997, I flipped through the phone book in my London hotel room, found the number I wanted, and lifted the receiver. Slowly and deliberately I punched the buttons on the dial and waited for someone to answer. A woman's voice soon responded: "National Museums of Scotland."

"I'd like to see the items belonging to Alexander Selkirk," I said. "I'm from Japan, and I'm ringing from London."

"Please wait while I connect your call," she said in a low, calm voice, and put me on hold.

I was back on the trail of Alexander Selkirk, in London this time. It was five years now since that short entry in *History of World Exploration* had first captivated me. In the interim I'd read widely about the man, traveled, given rein to my imagination. When puzzled I pored over the literature again or ransacked memories of my travels. I formed a hypothesis about where Selkirk might have lived on the island and tested it by conducting on-site explorations. Through it all, I was able to gain a real-life perspective on the life and adventures of this man buried in history, the prototypical Crusoe. But I wasn't finished yet: now I had to find out what became of him after his rescue, how he spent the remaining years of his life.

To accomplish this, I wanted to locate his will and personal possessions, as a window on his life. But tracking down the property of a man dead three centuries would not be easy. In the plane on the way to England, I told myself that this trip was a gamble. I did have some leads, but there was no guarantee that any of my information was reliable.

On arriving in London, I holed up in my hotel and made a series of phone calls. A 1939 book entitled *The Real Robinson Crusoe* by R. L. Mégroz—also the author of a BBC radio script based on Selkirk's adventures—mentioned that Selkirk's will was kept in Somerset House, but that proved not to be true. The elderly curator gave me a couple of suggestions on where to look, first at the Public Record Office on Chancery Lane, then at the Greater London Record Office (revamped to the London Metropolitan Archive in 1997) on Northampton Road. During my entire stay, however, I found no sign of the will's location or its existence.

I returned to Japan empty-handed, but word soon came from a representative of the Public Record Office that the will had been found. Eagerly I dashed off a reply and was able to obtain a copy of it at last.

Selkirk's relics, meanwhile, were reportedly being housed in the Scottish Antiquarian Museum, but that search also proved tricky. The name sounded fishy to me, for one thing. For all I knew, one of the many antique stores in England was grandiosely calling itself a museum. This suspicion sidetracked me for awhile, but in the end I found myself dealing with the National Museums of Scotland, with which the other museum had apparently merged some years back.

I stayed on hold quite some time, receiver pressed to my ear, waiting for my call to be put through. Finally a young-sounding male voice came on.

"I've been told your collection has a cup carved out of a coconut shell and a wooden sea chest used by Alexander Selkirk during his life on a deserted island," I said.

"That's right," the voice promptly confirmed.

"I've flown all the way from Japan to see them," I went on, adding that, if possible, I'd like to proceed to Edinburgh the following day.

With a promise to check on the items' whereabouts, he put me back on hold, soon returning with the information that the items were in storage and that if I wanted to come see them I was most welcome. Luck was turning my way.

I asked his name and arranged to meet him the next morning in the first-floor lobby of the National Museums of Scotland. Then I hung up and went out to buy a plane ticket to Edinburgh.

When I awoke the next morning, it was snowing. London at 6:00 A.M. was pitch black, against which the snowflakes and my own breath appeared all the whiter. I took the subway to Heathrow and boarded the shuttle for Edinburgh alongside attaché case–carrying businessmen.

I arrived at the lobby of the National Museums of Scotland at 10:00 sharp and went directly to the reception desk, where I introduced myself and said I had an appointment to see Dr. Caldwell. Soon a slender man with a full beard came out. Behind his glasses were eyes of distinctive calm and intelligence, and when he spoke, his choice of words was polite and well considered.

In addition to being the museum director, Dr. Caldwell had planned and produced a display on Alexander Selkirk in 1983 and was continuing to investigate his life and times. I learned a lot from him, and he, in turn, having never been to Robinson Crusoe Island, listened avidly to my tale. I was amazed and delighted to find another man who shared my passion.

"I really think Selkirk would have built his shelter out of stone, not wood. You have to remember, he had been brought up in Scotland and all he knew were stone houses."

Up to that point, I hadn't doubted the old document that had led me to believe that Selkirk's hut had been wooden. Now, I began to consider the influence of his Scottish upbringing in detail and the effects it might have had on his time on the island.

I was delighted to have actually met Dr. Caldwell in person, after five years of intensive research—we had much to talk to about.

To continue where I left off telling the story of Selkirk's miraculous life, let us go back to the day of his rescue in 1709. That day brought Selkirk face to face with someone from his past. When he boarded the English privateer vessel *Duke*, he spotted someone vaguely familiar—an old man with none of the air of authority of his younger days. Selkirk searched his memory, staring at the man's time-ravaged face. Was it true? Could this be him? It had to be a dream. Standing before him was Captain William Dampier, captain of the other vessel on that ill-fated voyage when Selkirk had been abandoned, four years and four months ago.

Dampier himself was staggered, having assumed Selkirk was long dead. With his shaggy hair and beard, and his face black with sunburn and grime, Selkirk too looked nothing like his former self. His ordeal had transformed him into a wily savage.

However great may have been Dampier's surprise, the shock felt by Selkirk at this unexpected reunion was many times greater. He learned that Dampier's ship the *St. George* had been seized by a Dutch vessel and its entire crew thrown into the brig before being shipped back to England. The galley *Cinque Ports*, which Selkirk had been on, sprang a leak after leaving him and very nearly sank before limping into harbor in New Granada (today's Colombia). There the men were captured and subjected to treatment so barbarous that all but six or seven died. Captain Stradling was among the survivors, but they remained at the mercy of the Spanish and nothing further was ever heard of them.

If Selkirk had not had that falling-out with the domineering Stradling, he would have been long dead.

Life and death on the high seas were as uncertain as a coin toss. The more Selkirk pondered, the more helpless he was to explain why he was still alive, why he had been safely rescued. It seemed too good to be true. Was it God who had intervened? In any case, the next chapter in his life was about to begin.

Captain Woodes Rogers's book contains this short but revealing statement: "Captain Dampier . . . told me that this was the best Man in [the *Cinque Ports*]; so I immediately agreed with him to be a Mate on board our Ship."

On the afternoon of February 14, 1709, the *Duke* and *Duchess* pulled anchor and left the Juan Fernandez Islands, proceeding on their pirating voyage. In addition to attacking merchant ships and seizing their cargoes, the two ships banded together to invade Spanish colonies as well. At 6:00 P.M. on April 21, they slipped upstream under cover of evening shadows and entered the city of Guayaquil in present-day Ecuador. Along the way, they captured ships and slaves and demanded ransom, turning their cannons toward the city in threat. This surprise attack completely paralyzed city defenses, allowing the marauders to plunder it at will.

The ships were so loaded down with booty that there was scarcely room to walk on deck. The rich spoils included precious metals, iron fittings, weapons, and rigging; cocoa, wheat, beans, rice, oil, and other foodstuffs; alcohol; clothing and dyes; and much, much more.

Yet not even this huge success was enough. The ships continued north to California, where they challenged a Spanish vessel to a fight. In the ensuing battle, Captain Rogers himself was injured by a bullet. In his own words, "I being shot through the left cheek, the bullet striking away great part of my upper jaw, and several teeth which dropt down on the deck where I fell." The vivid language befits a pirate captain's tale of derring-do.

After that, the ships left the Americas behind and proceeded due west, crossing the Pacific by way of Guam and Batavia (now Jakarta) and reaching the Cape of Good Hope, southernmost tip of the African continent, by the end of 1710. There they stayed for five months, arriving back in Ellis, London, at the mouth of the Thames, on October 14, 1711. Their three-year circumnavigation of the globe was a sweeping success.

The plundered goods were valued at some eight hundred thousand pounds, of which Selkirk, who had been promoted to sailing master during the voyage, was entitled to eight hundred pounds—a grand sum, equivalent to twenty years' pay for artisans like his father.

From 1711 to 1713 the record is spotty, though Selkirk's will indicates that in 1711 he lodged with a Mr. and Mrs. Mason in Covent Garden. Also, he was definitely in Bristol in 1713, where court records show that on September 23 he was summoned for drunken assault of one Richard Nettle.

In spring of the following year, Selkirk finally returned home to Largo, twelve years after leaving for having caused a minor fracas. The villagers, having long since given him up for dead, greeted his return less with joy and relief than with outright shock. When the shock wore off they embraced him warmly, but Selkirk could no longer blend in. The hometown he had yearned for with such intensity was not the way he remembered it at all. He felt wretched and let down. His parents were in good health, but they had aged, and he found them very different from the mother and father of his memory. His old friends were all married with children, living peaceful, happy lives; their faces bore no sign of the cheeky pranksters they once were.

In 1712, Captain Rogers published his *A Cruising Voyage round the World* and his aide, Captain Edward Cooke (not the famous explorer), published *A Voyage to the South Sea and round the World*. Both men included mention of Selkirk's rescue. Getting wind of the incident, essayist Richard Steele interviewed Selkirk in London and published his strange tale in *The Englishman* of December 3, 1713:

> *The person I speak of is Alexander Selkirk, whose name is familiar to men of curiosity, from the fame of his having lived four years and four months alone in the Island of Juan Fernandez. I had the pleasure frequently, to converse with the man soon after his arrival in England in the year 1711. It was a matter of great curiosity to hear him, as he is a man of good sense, give an account of the different revolutions in his own mind in that long solitude. . . . When I first saw him I thought if I had not been let into his character and story I could have discerned that he had been much separated from company from his aspect and gesture; there was a strong but cheerful seriousness in his look, and a certain disregard to the ordinary things around him, as if he had been sunk in thought. . . . The man frequently bewailed his return to the world, which could not, he said, with all its enjoyments, restore to him the tranquillity of its solitude.[1]*

---

1. R. L. Mégroz, *The Real Robinson Crusoe* (London: The Cresset Press, 1939), pp. 193–97.

All these rescue stories won over public opinion, and Selkirk's incredible adventures and miraculous return home were the talk of the nation. He became an instant celebrity.

But John Howell's *The Life and Adventures of Alexander Selkirk,* based on information from Selkirk's immediate family and relatives as well as the Largo Parish Church, makes it clear that Selkirk found all this attention distasteful. He had no wish to be famous and have total strangers addressing him with old-boy familiarity. The more people fussed over him, the more constrained he felt; the more he was lionized, the more he shut himself off from society. In the end he dug a cave in his garden, where he would hole himself up in complete isolation. He also bought a boat and took to rowing out into the Firth of Forth for the day, returning home as late as possible.

The old Alexander Selkirk, fleet runner of woodlands and powerful swimmer of seas, was nowhere to be found. His behavior became increasingly chaotic and incoherent. Unable to adapt to society, no longer sure of the meaning or value of his life, Selkirk felt alienated from his very birthplace. Another passage in Steele's essay in *The Englishman* preserves for us his plaintive voice: "I am now worth eight hundred pounds, but shall never be so happy as when I was not worth a farthing."

The only one who gave Selkirk hope was a woman named Sophia Bruce who worked on a farm at Keil's Den and became his close confidante and supporter. Drawn by her genuine beauty, he came to feel the torments of an irrepressible love.

Sophia's parents knew Selkirk, but they were not at all happy that their daughter was seeing him. A man with no trade who spent his days lolling around the house was not a fit human being, let alone a matrimonial catch; his attentions would only wind up making their daughter miserable. But such opposition only fanned the couple's passion, and finally they decided to elope. One day they left Largo behind and set off together for London.

Just at that time, the revolution and turbulence of recent years had at last quieted down, and hopes for a new era were burgeoning across the nation. Of London itself, it was well said that "When a man is tired of London, he is tired of life; for there is in London all that life can afford" (1777, quoted in Boswell's *The Life of Samuel Johnson*), and the city was indeed overflowing with marvels. The yearly grand market featured a wide assortment of street performances, with acrobatics, stunts, puppet shows, and more. Stalls and roadside stands stood crowded side by side. With so much to do, one could easily spend all day—better yet, all week—wandering there and never want to go home.

London Tower offered the public a rare view of creatures from every corner of the globe: lions, panthers, ostriches, bears, hyenas, giraffes. Children and adults alike were riveted by the display of living curiosities, and the zoological garden was thronged from morning till night.

Public houses were another essential part of Londoners' lives in the eighteenth century. There, you could not only order gin and other strong liquors over the counter but also join in games and singing or see sporting events like cricket or boxing matches. You might even talk over the place and time for an animal baiting game. London pubs were centers of socializing and recreation.

For country girl Sophia Bruce, everything in the city of London was fresh and sensational. Selkirk, on the other hand, spent his days soaked in gin. As he hung out in pubs, his consciousness in a haze, all that made him feel truly alive were his memories of life alone on the island. The greater the trial he'd suffered, the more shining the memory. He remembered it all: his excitement the first day he succeeded in making a fire, and his surge of confidence after building a hut; the pageant of the seasons over stream and hill, and above it all, the all-seeing sky. The only place where he could relive it all, ruminating countless times over his memories, was seated in a pub, drunk on strong gin.

It wasn't long before a crack developed in the shared outlook of Sophia Bruce and Alexander Selkirk, one that grew steadily larger as time went on. The pleasantness of life together could not go on indefinitely. Eventually Selkirk came to his senses. What was he doing? This was not the life for him. He belonged back at sea.

To Sophia, the idea that Selkirk would ever be a sailor again was unbelievable. Surely of all men that had ever lived, her Alexander had tasted most fully the dangers, trials, and suffering sea voyages entailed. Why must he go back to the accursed sea, leaving her alone? What did the sea offer him? Tears in her eyes, she asked the question over and over, but the answer was unfathomable.

In 1717, Selkirk signed up on the HMS *Enterprise.* The will he wrote before setting sail gives a moving picture of his frame of mind at that juncture of his life, and of his love for Sophia.

In the name of God, Amen, I, Alexander Selkirk of Largo, in the shire of Fife, in North Brittaine, marriner, being now bound out on a voyage to sea, but calling to minde the perrills and dangers of the seas, and other uncertaintys of this transitory life, doe, for avoyding controversies and disputes which may happen to arise after my decease, make, publish, and declare this my last will and testament, in manner and form following, (that is to say), first and principly I recommend my soul into the hands of Almighty God that gave it, hopeing for the salvation thereof through the alone merritts, death, and sufferings of my Lord and Saviour Jesus Christ; and my body I commit to the earth or sea, as it shall please God in his infinite wisdom to order and direct; and as for and concerning that portion of this world, which the Lord hath been pleased to lend unto me, I give and dispose thereof as follows (viz.) Item, I give and bequeath unto my loveing friend, Katherine Mason, the wife of John Mason of the parish of Covent-Garden, merchant-taylor, the sume of tenn pounds of good and lawful money of Great Brittaine, to be paid her within twelve months after my decease. Item, I give and bequeath unto my loveing and wellbeloved friend, Sophia Bruce of the Pelmel, London, spinster, all and singular my lands, tenements, out-houses, gardens, yards, orchards, situate, lyeing , and being in Largo aforesaid, or in any other place or places whatsoever, during her natural life, and noe longer; and at and after her decease I hereby give, devise, and bequeath the same unto my loving nephew, Alexander Silkirk, sone of David Silkirk of Largo aforesaid, tanner, &c., and to his heirs or assignes. Item, my will and minde is, and I hereby declare it so to be, that my honoured father, John Silkirk, should have and enjoy the eastermost house on the Craggy Wall in Largo aforesaid for and dureing his naturall life, and have and receive the rents, issues, and profitts thereof, to his owne propper use; and that after his decease it should fall into the hands of the said Sophia Bruce, and so into the hands of my said loveing nephew, Alexander Silkirk, in case he outlive my said loveing friend, Sophia Bruce; and as for and concerning all and singular the rest, residue, and remainder of my sallery, wages, goods, weres, profitts, merchandizes, sume and sumes of money, gold, silver, *wearing apparel, as well linnen and woolen, and all other my effects whatsoever, as well debt outstanding either by bond, bill, book, accompt, or otherwise, as any other thing whatsoever, which shall be due, owing, payable, and belonging or in any-wise of right appertaining unto me at the time of my decease, and not herein otherwise disposed of; I hereby give, devise, and bequeath the same unto my said loveing friend, Sophia Bruce, and to her heires and assignes for ever; and I doe hereby nominate, make, elect, and appoint, my said trusty and loveing friend, sophia Bruce, full and sole executrix of this my last will and testament; hereby revoaking and makeing voyd and of none effect all former and other wills, testaments, and deeds of gift whatsoever by me, at any time or times heretofore made, and I doe ordain and ratifie these presents, and no other, to stand and be for, and as my only last will and testament; in witness whereof, to this my said will, I, the said testator, Alexander Silkirk, have hereunto set my hand and seale the thirteenth day of January,* ann. Domini *1717, and in the 4th year of King George, &c.*

Alexander Selkirk

Signed, sealed, published, and declared, by the testator, for his last will and testament, in the presence of

Alexander Bushan.
Sarah Holman.

Exactly how many years Selkirk spent in Largo after his rescue it is impossible to say, but this will indicates that he had become a man of great property. Considering that when he first came back he lived huddled in a cave, it is clear that he had managed to amass considerable money from his fame and had invested it wisely.

Selkirk signed the will, and went off again to sea.

On April 25, 1719, the publishing house of William Taylor released Daniel Defoe's magnificent novel *The Life and Adventures of Robinson Crusoe,* based in part on published accounts of Selkirk's story. The full title of the novel, incidentally, is much more elaborate: *The Life and Strange Surprizing Adventures of Robinson Crusoe, of York, Mariner: who lived eight and twenty years, all alone in an un-inhabited island on the coast of America, near the mouth of the great river of Oroonoque; having been cast on shore by shipwreck, where on all the men perished but himself. With an account how he was at last as strangely deliver'd by pyrates. Written by Himself.* Until he wrote this prodigiously-titled novel at age fifty-nine, Defoe was known not as a novelist but as a journalist. He was born in 1660, in the parish of St. Giles's, Cripplegate, London, the third child and oldest son of tallow chandler James Foe. (The name was changed to Defoe sometime after 1695.) He died alone on April 24, 1731, at the age of seventy-one, in a rented room in Ropemaker's Alley, London.

Defoe lived during an age of revolution, and his own life fully reflected the stormy times. The child of a Puritan, he was forced to attend the small academy at Newington Green, as Nonconformists were unable to send their children to Oxford or Cambridge. The academy was to have a decided influence on the course of Defoe's life. Rather than immersing him in erudite Latin, that staple of the classical education taught in ivory-tower universities, it gave him a broad and practical education with emphasis on living languages: English and French.

Jonathan Swift, author of *Gulliver's Travels,* later called Defoe "illiterate" and Defoe reportedly struck back, disparaging those who were educated in the university but did not understand practical learning (like modern languages, science, and geography)—an interesting exchange reflective of the social conditions. It is ironic that *Gulliver's Travels* and *Robinson Crusoe* are sometimes paired together as masterpieces of fiction for young people.

On graduation from the academy, Defoe went into business as a merchant, selling socks and knitwear, wine and brandy, tobacco and other commodities. He prospered and soon grew wealthy. Not long after setting up in business he married Mary Tuffley, the daughter of a winemaker, who bore him eight children.

Nine years after he got started in business, Defoe suddenly went bankrupt. One important reason was that England went to war with France and Louis XIV, and Defoe's ships were seized—although some point to Defoe's lack of caution and interest in politics as root causes of the setback.

In any case, the losses he sustained only sharpened his appetite for political involvement, and in 1694 he wrote a suggestion for raising money for the war with France (1689–97) that won approval from the government. From then on, he devoted himself to writing pamphlet after pamphlet. Satirical, solidly middle-class in perspective, and written in a simple, easily understandable prose, Defoe's essays reflected the voice of the people, and they made him a star.

Once after being arrested as the author of an ironic pamphlet entitled "The Shortest Way with the Dissenters" that ridiculed the government, he was sentenced to three days in pillory, but the mob rallied to his support and even strewed him with garlands. The degree of his popularity is evident, given that it was not uncommon for men in pillory to be pelted with raw eggs, roughed up, or even killed at the hands of the mob.

After his release from Newgate Prison, in February 1704 Defoe founded a weekly periodical, the *Review*. This remarkable achievement established his credentials as a premier journalist. Caught between the progovernment, aristocratic High-Church Tories and the Whig party, which upheld the power of Parliament against the crown and was supported by the landed gentry and town merchants, he remained active as a journalist for fifteen more years before writing his first work of fiction, *Robinson Crusoe*.

Looking at his life overall, it is clear that this work was no mere product of coincidence. Though written in the form of a novel, it brilliantly captures the worldview of the middle-class man. And it was inevitable that Defoe would be drawn to the story of Selkirk, a Presbyterian like himself who was raised as the son of a tanner.

From the beginning, *Robinson Crusoe* was hugely popular. As soon as it appeared in bookstores, this tale of a shipwrecked man caused a sensation, and several tens of thousands of copies sold out immediately. Martin Green, in his book *The Robinson Crusoe Story*, describes the novel's tremendous success as follows.

> *The success of* Robinson Crusoe *was immediate. There were seven reprints in London in seven years; it was serialized within the first year and pirated, abridged, adapted, and dramatized endlessly. It was translated into French in 1720, and the translation was reprinted in 1721, 1722, and 1726; the Dutch trans-*

*lation was reprinted in 1721, 1736, 1752, and 1791. The great-
est interest was shown in Germany, where a great number of books
were issued with "Robinson Crusoe" in their titles. Some of them
had been written and even published before 1719, but were reis-
sued to cash in on the enthusiasm for Defoe's book. Some were famous and important in their own right. Both* Gil Blas *and* Don
Quixote *appeared in German as, respectively, the Spanish and
the Schwaebische Robinson.*[2]

Adults welcomed the book as a great story, while children found a new hero. Pious folk saw Robinson Crusoe
as the embodiment of Puritan ideals, and politicians used
him as a symbol for activities of middle-class citizenry.
Businessmen in the throes of the Industrial Revolution,
which was only then beginning to gear up, embraced
Robinson Crusoe enthusiastically as someone who built a
solid foundation for a comfortable life through slow,
painstaking labor.

The novel had enormous impact not only on the
masses but also on thinkers in many disparate fields as
well, including Adam Smith, Karl Marx, Max Weber, and
Henri Bergson. In "Émile," his famous essay on education, Enlightenment thinker Jean-Jacques Rousseau
wrote:

*I hate books . . . [but] . . . since we must have books, there is one
book which, to my thinking, supplies the best treatise on an education according to nature. This is the first book Emile will read;
for a long time it will form his whole library, and it will always
retain an honoured place. It will be the text to which all our talks
about natural science are but the commentary. It will serve to test*

---

2. Martin Green, *The Robinson Crusoe Story* (University Park: Penn-
sylvania State University Press, 1990), p. 20.

our progress towards a right judgment, and it will always be read with delight, so long as our taste is unspoiled. What is this wonderful book? Is it Aristotle? Pliny? Buffon? No; it is Robinson Crusoe.[3]

Yet by now, five years after his miraculous return to civilization, Alexander Selkirk was no longer a figure of public interest. As the novel became the talk of the nation, the man on whose story it was based had faded from view, forgotten.

On January 8, 1997, in Edinburgh's National Museums of Scotland, Dr. David Caldwell and I threaded our way through a maze of corridors until we reached an office. Low-hanging leaden clouds, framed in the window, reminded me that I was indeed in Scotland. Two museum workers sat soundlessly in the center of the room, busy at their desks. When I gave a slight bow, they broke into warm smiles.

Dr. Caldwell took a small box out of a locker and laid it gently on the table. Then he handed me a pair of thin rubber gloves, like those a surgeon wears for an operation. I followed his instructions without a word. At last, I was going to encounter articles Selkirk had used during his life on the uninhabited island. I could feel my heart pounding. An encounter with a man's personal possessions was in a sense an encounter with the man himself. These things had ridden the waves of time to appear here before me; surely they would speak vol-

---

3. Green, *The Robinson Crusoe Story,* pp. 40–41.

umes about Selkirk's life centuries ago on that deserted island.

When I had finished putting on the gloves, Dr. Caldwell carefully opened the small box.

The National Museums of Scotland presently owns two of Selkirk's possessions, both of which had passed through the hands of family and friends. One is a cup carved from a coconut shell, the other a big, wooden chest. The cup is shaped like a long-stemmed wineglass. How it came into Selkirk's possession is unknown. Did he carve it himself to while away the hours on a long voyage? Or was it a war trophy, seized off the coast of Africa or on the Pacific Ocean? Even in Selkirk's day, a coconut cup was a great rarity.

To celebrate his return, the mouth and inside bottom of the cup were inlaid with silver. Around the rim is a silver band inscribed, "The Cup of Alexander Selkirk, 1704–9, in Juan Fernandez."

Yet stare as I would, I could detect no sign in the cup of the miseries of Selkirk's island life. It must not have been for everyday use, I decided. Polished to a soft shine, remarkably free of nicks and scratches, it had an elegant dignity.

I tried to imagine Selkirk ceremonially drinking water from this cup on special occasions. How did it taste? I wondered. And what sort of occasions might they have been? No doubt any pleasurable occurrence—however small—that broke the monotony of his melancholy life was reason enough for him to delight his eyes with the cup's smoothly carved zigzag design.

The chest, covered all over with scratches, was another matter. Despite its worn appearance, it was sturdily built and must have been sheltered from the elements, for it had suffered no serious damage. Selkirk likely had used it to store his bullets, gunpowder, and other precious possessions—perhaps even the cup. A sharp metal tool had been used to inscribe the heavy lid with his initials and service number: "A.S. No. 34."

Above all, the chest persuaded me that Selkirk must have lived in Cumberland after all. According to articles I had read, some people imagined him holing up for the first few months of his exile in a cave in Puerto Inglés and later moving to Cumberland to build himself a proper hut. One look at the chest, however, told me that any idea of him hauling it over steep mountainous terrain was unrealistic. Nor was there any sign of its having been dragged along the ground for miles, either. That settled it in my mind: the cave was deliberately enlarged in later years to make it look plausible as his island headquarters, although possibly Selkirk may have come across it at some point and used it as a shelter.

As I studied the empty wooden chest, darkened by the intervening centuries, I couldn't help wondering aloud if any other items used by Selkirk on the island might still exist. Dr. Caldwell answered my simple question in an offhanded way.

"Although there are questions about the provenance, his musket is in the possession of one of his descendants." He handed me a copy of a fascinating article entitled "On the Crusoe Gun Trail" by Richard Wilson, published in the May 1986 issue of *Scotman Magazine* (vol. 7, no. 2).

After trying to recall something, Dr Caldwell added, "Yes, and I believe his knife and powder horn are in a museum in Kirkcaldy."

I seized on the words, having already explored the history of Selkirk's musket. Dr. Caldwell kindly arranged over the telephone for me to see the knife and powder horn, instructing the museum curator to remove the articles from the safe so that a "young man from Japan" could have a look at them that very day. As it turned out, the two venerable items had been removed to another town. As I listened to Dr. Caldwell make the arrangements, my palms grew sweaty and my chest pounded. It came down to a battle against time.

I checked my watch. There were a dozen minutes till 1:00 P.M. In order to get back to London that day, I would have to make it to the airport by 5:00 sharp. That gave me barely four hours to make this side trip. Would it be enough?

Dr. Caldwell told me what to do: take a taxi from the museum to Waverley Station in Edinburgh, board a train for Inverness and get off at Lucas, then race to St. Andrews Museum by taxi again. Half grasping what was involved, I stared at a map while he rang the station. He banged down the receiver and barked, "You won't make it if you don't get a move on!" There was one train per hour, and the next left at ten past one. I had exactly fifteen minutes. The chance was too good to miss. Thanking Dr. Caldwell profusely, I rushed out the door.

In the taxi, and then on the poky local train, I could think of nothing but the disappearing minutes. But thankfully all went well, and I arrived at the museum to find the articles already laid out for my inspection.

Selkirk's jackknife. The heavy feel of it in my palm stirred my imagination. The blade was gone, the metal bits attached to the handle crumbling with rust. The handle itself was carved from animal horn and decorated with a lattice design. Slowly I closed my hand around it in a tight grip, realizing then that the design was no mere decoration but kept the knife from slipping.

How many dozen goats had he skinned and dismembered with this knife? He'd used it to clean fish, build huts. The weight of it in my hand sent my thoughts skimming over land and sea to that far-away island where I too had lived. I could see it all vividly—the hills and valleys, the luma trees, the streams, even the little stones alongside them.

The knife spoke tellingly of Selkirk's ordeals, but the powder horn seemed much more refined and even elegant. Made of wood, it was carved and finished to resemble animal horn and branded with a strange geometric design. It was well preserved, suggesting that after he ran out of gunpowder Selkirk kept it shut away inside the chest.

I was well pleased with the fruits of my trip to Scotland.

On the way back to London, I looked through the article about the mysterious story of Selkirk's gun.

In tracking down the musket Selkirk brought back with him from the island, the author wrote letters to various people, went to meet with them in person, and enlisted the aid of museum directors and gun specialists. I will summarize his findings.

While Selkirk used only one gun during his life on the island, auction records and memories of different owners indicate that more than one gun has been believed to be his over the years.

First, gun number one: According to a newspaper cutting dated May 22, 1924, "the Robinson Crusoe gun" was auctioned off by Sotheby's in London. Records indicate that the buyer was C. J. Sawyer, a rare book dealer on London's Grafton Street. At some time in the mid 1920s he took the gun to Colet Court, the prep school his son attended, and gave a lecture to the students about the real Robinson Crusoe. What became of the gun after that is unknown, except that it was apparently sold to someone in America.

Gun number two: In 1905, the local laird decided to sell Selkirk's gun at Dowell's auction house in Edinburgh. David Gillies, Allan Jardine's great-grandfather and the man who put up the statue of Selkirk, heard about the plan and headed for Edinburgh, but as luck would have it his train was late and he was helpless to stop the sale. The gun was sold to Mrs. Hulda Whyte of Philadelphia. She later sold it to Louis Schmidt, manager of Ostendorff's restaurant in Philadelphia. Allegedly, it hung on the wall of the restaurant until 1926 after which Schmidt gave it to the mayor of the city, who in turn gave it to the British ambassador for it to be handed over to "the Daniel Defoe museum" in England. No one knows what became of it after that.

Gun number three: According to Florence Osbourn of East Dereham, Norfolk, her husband bought Selkirk's gun in a Newmarket antique shop around 1953. After that, it apparently passed into the possession of a Selkirk descendant for a time, but whether or not this is the gun Allan Jardine told me about remains unclear.

Each of the guns has carved on the butt in large letters one of the following: "A. SELKIRK," or "SEALGRAIG" or "ALEXR. SELKIRK," along with the date "1705." From photographs of the guns, it appears that each one is a different model. It is an extraordinary story made possible by the auction system. The story about Selkirk's gun is cloaked in the veil of history.

The following morning I went to the Public Record Office in Kew, on the outskirts of London. Old documents relating to the British navy were kept there, and I wanted to see if I could find the log of the HMS *Weymouth* on what was Selkirk's last sea voyage.

It was an hour's ride to Kew from the city center. I dozed while the train carried me past London's old streets and got off at quiet Kew Station. The Public Record Office there had only recently been completed; as I stared up at the building in the freezing wind, it looked like a gigantic iceberg.

I signed in at the entrance and showed my passport, after which my personal data were promptly entered on a digital disk and I was issued a reader's ticket with a bar code. This display of twentieth-century technology only made the task of searching for information about a document from the 1700s all the more daunting.

I went upstairs to the reference room and told a librarian the theme of my research and what I was hoping to find. Glancing around, I couldn't help noticing that everyone was glued fast to their desks, scowling. The tension in the air was infectious.

With the librarian at my side to guide me, I began searching for the log of the HMS *Weymouth*, c. 1720. I was prepared for there to be endless complications in retrieving one antique document from a vast store of materials, but all I had to do was look up the ship's name and date in an index and input the necessary information into the computer. Then I was given a small pager to hold and told to report to the counter when it went off.

After twenty minutes the pager started to beep. Half disbelieving, I went over to the counter and picked up a stout box covered in blue fabric and bound with string. I took it into the reading room and began to open it. When I undid the string, a tiny cloud of dust rose in the air. Inside was another box. I opened it and caught my breath at the ancient pages lying in front of me.

Yellowed all over, the paper was corroded in spots and had holes in it. Its black ink had smeared. The pages gave off the same smell of aging paper and ink that fills antique book shops. This was no replica, this was the actual daily log of a ship's voyage from England to Africa in the 1720s. It began in February 1719 and ended on April 25, 1722, with a complete record for the days in between of weather, wind direction, and position at sea, as well as any notable actions or events. It was kept by Bryant Twiselton.

Selkirk boarded the HMS *Enterprise* on March 4, 1717, having made out his will as sailors commonly did before a long sea voyage, and arrived back in England some eight months later. Less than a year afterward, he set out on another voyage. In August 1718 he boarded the HMS *Weymouth* as mate.

After leaving London, the *Weymouth* spent the next two years proceeding slowly from Woolwich at the mouth of the River Thames down to Sheerness, Portsmouth, and Plymouth. Getting from London to Plymouth on the Cornwall Peninsula, jutting out sharply at the southwest extremity of the British Isles, does not normally take two years. As if sensing the fate that would befall its crew, the ship lingered close to home, seemingly loath to set out on the open seas.

In November 1720, still anchored at Plymouth, the *Weymouth* took on board water, biscuits, corned beef, beef, pork, peas, oatmeal, butter, and fifteen cheeses. Not even then did she set sail, remaining at anchor for another whole month. The will that Alexander Selkirk wrote during that interval is still on file in the Public Record Office. Did he have any idea what consequences it would brew?

In the Name of God, Amen, I Alexander Silkirk of Oarston within the P^rish of Plymstock in the County of Devon Mate of his Maj^ties Shipp Weymouth being in bodily Health, and of sound and disposeing Mind and Memory, and considering the Perils and Dangers of the Seas, and other uncertainties of this Transitory Life, do for avoiding Controversies after my Decease, Make, Publish and declare this my last Will and Testament in manner following. (That is to say) First I recommend my Soul to God that gave it, and my Body I commit to the Earth or Sea as it shall please God to Order; and as or and concerning all my Worldly Estate, I give, and Bequeath, and Dispose thereof as followeth. (That is to say) All such Wages, Sum and Sums of Money, Lands, Tenements, Goods, Chattels and Estate whatsoever, as shall be in any ways due, owing or belonging to me at the Time of my Decease, I do Give, Devise and Bequeath the same unto my welbeloved wife Frances Silkirk of Oarston afores^d & her Assignes forever.

And I do hereby Nominate and Appoint my sd wife Frances the whole and sole Executrix of this my last Will and Testament hereby Revoking all former and other Wills, Testaments and Deeds of Gift by me at any Time heretofore made: And I do Or-

dain and Ratify these presents to Stand and be for my only last Will and Testament. In Witness whereof to this my said Will, I have set my Hand and Seal the Twelfth Day of December Annoq. Dom. 1720 and in the Seventh year of the Reign of his Majesty King George over Great Britain, &c.

Alexr Selkirk

Signed Sealed and Published,
in the Presence of us,
Step Turtleff
Will Warren
Sam Bury Notie: Publiq

Finally the HMS *Weymouth* set sail across the Atlantic, heading south and arriving in January 1721 at the Madeira Islands off the coast of Morocco. On March 31, she dropped anchor off Saint Mary Island, at the mouth of the River Gambia in west Africa. Strong winds, fog, and intermittent rain kept her confined there for several days.

On April 2, 1721, Selkirk's name appears in the log for the first time.

Winds, NW, W, to NNW. Grounded on a sand call'd the middle ground (Cape St. Marie). Modr. and fair at 4 p.m. Anch^d in 5 fath. water at Pt. Mary. Mr. Barnsly took the first Mate (Mr. Selkerk) with him and went a sounding the Depth of water this morn: the Boates was sent to lay on the sands by directions of Mr. Selkirk wch being done at ½ p^t 7, weigh'd in order to goe into the River. Standing in between the boates where the ship at 9 struck the ground we laid all a-back but the ship stuck fast . . .

On May 31, 1721, they arrived at the Gold Coast, or what is now the coast of the Republic of Ghana; repeated contact with the local people, the men mostly for cheap labor and the women mostly for sex, resulted in a virulent infectious disease spreading aboard the ship. From then on, the log entries grow brief and sporadic:

July 11 Mr. White, Purser, deceased.
July 14 Mr. Peine, Schoolmaster, deceased.

The log records a living hell. Sickness was endemic, death a mundane, daily affair. Soon all details are omitted, with only the dead man's name followed by the word "deceased" or "died" or "died this day" scrawled on the page, as above. Plainly, the living were weak with exhaustion

It was summer right at the equator, with continual rain and humidity, raging disease, and huge swarms of malarial mosquitoes. Day by day and month by month, shipboard conditions worsened.

Tough as he was, even Selkirk fell victim to the epidemic. He developed a high fever, lost his appetite, and grew steadily weaker, able to do nothing but lie in bed in his cabin and groan. Now and then he regained consciousness long enough to see dimly that someone was bringing him water or chilled soup, but he said nothing. When a monsoon hit and stormy waves threatened to engulf the ship, the interior was hushed, in contrast to nature's spiraling fury. Now no one came to his cabin anymore.

One by one the members of the crew died. Each time, the living hauled the body away. At first there were cries of grief and sorrow, but as the death toll mounted, the men grew stoical. Selkirk could no longer make out sounds of weeping.

Where had he come from, and where was he headed? . . .

As he slipped gradually into a coma, Selkirk looked back on his life. One by one, images formed and vanished in his mind of all the people he had ever known and of the peaceful, vibrant scenery on the island of Mas-a-Tierra.

On December 13, 1721, one of the sailors found Selkirk lying cold in his bed. His death is recorded simply in the log of the *Weymouth*, which was anchored that day off Cape Coast, Ghana.

Alexr. Selkirk, DD.
P.M. Alexr. Selkirk Deceased.

There is no mention of a cause of death, but it is thought likely that he died of yellow fever, the scourge of sailors along the coast of Africa in those days.

In the heavy fog, when the black silhouette of a ship appeared over the horizon, people wondered if it was a floating wreck. The ship seemed to make little headway and her sails were ragged, with no sign of mending. None but a few curious souls bothered to meet her at the dock. Two years after starting out, the *Weymouth* limped back in a cheerless homecoming that perfectly matched the horrible time she had been through.

Still known as the "Dark Continent," Africa was becoming better known along its coastline, but the inland areas remained full of mystery—and heading into the Gulf of Guinea for slave trafficking meant taking your life in your hands. The intermittent tropical low-pressure areas and blustering squalls, with air temperatures at or near the warmth of human skin and humidity like a steam bath, sapped the sailors' strength and spirits. Malaria and yellow fever ran wild. One by one, sturdy sailors were taken sick and died, as the living hung precariously to life.

Among the many victims this time was Alexander Selkirk. Held in awe by his peers for his unparalleled feat of survival, Selkirk was virtually forgotten by society at large; those few who remembered him were not likely to feel overcome with sentiment at news of his death. His passing aroused no general stir. Word passed quietly from his surviving shipmates to friends and acquaintances, and finally to his family.

In July 1722, soon after the *Weymouth* returned home, a woman calling herself Frances Selkirk applied in court to have the will of Alexander Selkirk probated. In accordance with the 1720 will naming her as executrix, Selkirk's remuneration for the voyage and his personal effects were to be left to her. The amount owed his estate after the disastrous voyage was very little—only forty pounds in all. Compared with the eight hundred pounds he had once earned privateering with Captain Rodgers, it was a trifling return for a huge effort.

Frances' application for probate was soon contested, however, and the case went to court. The plaintiff was Sophia Bruce, executrix of Selkirk's 1717 will. Sophia stated that she had married Alexander Selkirk on January 13, 1717, registering her complaint in the name Sophia Selcraig. She claimed that the later will should be invalidated as Selkirk had written it in a state of heavy intoxication. Frances, meanwhile, pointed out that Sophia had lived with Alexander without the blessing of the church and denounced her as a woman of easy virtue. Looking back on Selkirk's stay in Plymouth, Frances recalled that he swore he was a bachelor, never married, and ardently sought her hand. She had hesitated to accept his proposal so soon before he was to go to sea, she said, but finally yielded and married him on December 12, 1720, in St. Andrews Parish Church in Plymouth, in a solemn Church of England service. The marriage record was on file in the church for anybody to see.

As soon as she learned of Selkirk's death, Frances remarried (her next husband was a Plymouth tallow chandler by the name of Hall) and set about seeking her rightful inheritance. In both the marriage record in St. Andrews Parish Church and the 1720 will, Selkirk had referred to Frances as his "welbeloved wife." Clearly, these facts were in her favor. Sophia, meanwhile, was described in the earlier will as "beloved friend" and lacked documentation of her supposed marriage; she did not have a single piece of evidence to support her case in court.

A verdict was reached no later than 1824. According to John Howell, who interviewed Selcraig descendants in the 1800s for his book *The Life and Adventures of Alexander Selkirk,* "a gay widow, by name Frances Candis or Candia, came to Largo to claim the property left to him by his father,—the house at the Craigie Well."[4]

Around the same time, Sophia wrote the following letter.

Sophia Selcraig's Petition to Mr. Say for Relief.
Reverend Sir,
I being a person much reduced to want, by reason of this hard season, makes me presume to trouble you, which I hope your good-

---

4. John Howell, *The Life and Adventures of Alexander Selkirk* (London: Oliver & Boyd, 1829), p. 134.

ness will not resist to relieve, I being the widow of Mr. Selchrig who was left four years and four months on the island of John Ferinanda; and besides I had three uncles in Scotland, all ministers, to wit, Mr. Harry Rymer, Mr. James Rymer, and another; therefore depending humbly on your prudent and wise consideration of my present circumstances, Revd Sir,

Your petitioner shall ever pray,

Sophia Selchrig[5]

After this, all word of her vanishes. Whether she continued to live in London or went back to Scotland, no one knows.

---

5. Mégroz, *The Real Robinson Crusoe*, pp. 173–74.

CHAPTER

Seven

The Legend

The following letter came not long after my return to Japan.

12 September 1997
Dear Mr. Takahashi
I hope you will find the enclosed document of interest. I got the copy from the Duke of Hamilton. It does not appear to be dated, but is a petition by Frances Selkirk, widow of Alexander, to the then Duke of Hamilton to have her husband's journal returned. She says this was the journal he kept while on Juan Fernandez ('Ferdinando') and that he gave it to the duke's father on his

return to England. It would be wonderful if the said journal, or
a copy of it, could be identified!

Yours sincerely
Dr. David H. Caldwell
Curator, Scottish Medieval Collections

Selkirk had kept a journal? The news was stunning.
Over and over, I reread the letter. Until now, lacking any
proof of a diary, I had dismissed the notion of one. Now I
held in my hands a copy of a letter from Frances Selkirk,
Alexander's widow, begging the return of her late husband's journal. It astounded me.

Here are the contents of her petition in full:

To His Grace the Duke of Hamilton re:
The most Humble Petition of Frances Selkirk
Most Humble Shosworth
That Yr Grace's Petition^r is the widdow of Alexander Selkirk who
was left on the desolate island called Ferdinando where he con-
tinued alone four years and four months all which time he kept a
journal of his observations as also of the Voyages he made with
Capt. Dempiore as also in the Duke which took the Aquaperlea
Ship in the South Sea which ship Yr. Petition^r's husband had in
his charge as Commander to bring to England and upon his ar-
rival his late Grace Yr most noble Father then desireing to see the
abovesaid journall of Petition^r's said Husband did leave it with
him after which, proceeding again to leave on another Voyage,
died in the same and Yr Grace's Petition^r being now reduced to
very low circumstances is advised that said journall would be of
some considerable advantage to her in her personal circumstances
and most humbly hopeing that it may have bin reserved safe in
the Library of Yr Most Noble Predecessor.

Therefore Yr Petition^r most humbly begs that Your Grace in Yr
Great Goodness would be pleased to condescend to give such di-

rections as thereby your Petition^r may have the said Journall De-
liver'd to her.

Assd Y^r Petition^r : as in duty bound for Y^r Grace shall ever
Pray.

I sat right down and wrote to Dr. Caldwell, eager to
know how he had discovered this old document. It
turned out to have been a complete coincidence. Apparently, a scholar came across it unexpectedly while going
through the family archives of the Duke of Hamilton in
Scotland. The petition had lain untouched for hundreds
of years.

This raised the possibility of other papers connected
with her petition being in the family archives, or indeed
of the diary itself quietly slumbering somewhere. Caldwell
commented, "I think if he still had the diary we should
know about it. I have asked a friend in the National Por-
trait Gallery who got a doctorate for research based on his
[the Duke of Hamilton's] papers, and she is sure she
never came across it."

He went on to make an unexpected suggestion. Since
this old paper from the duke's family archives offered
tangible proof of the existence of a journal kept by
Selkirk, it would be worthwhile investigating the diary
now in the hands of Selkirk's descendants. Theirs might
be a completely different diary or—if not the real thing
itself—a copy or facsimile of the journal mentioned in
this petition.

A descendant of Alexander Selkirk was in possession of
a document that was just possibly Selkirk's diary: as soon
as I heard this, I sent off a letter asking permission to see
the manuscript. As it happened, this was not my first contact with the lady. Back when I was pursuing Selkirk's
musket, I had called her and begged for a chance to see

the one in her possession—only to be turned down. I had no reason to believe my chances were any better this time.

There was a legend associated with Selkirk's diary. A century or more after his death, his name and the memory of his very existence had passed into oblivion. Then on March 1, 1851, the *Bristol Mirror* carried a letter to the editor that caught the public fancy, catapulting Selkirk back into the limelight. The theory that the fictional Robinson Crusoe was based on Selkirk, which the letter supports, was the stuff of high drama.

To the Editor of the Bristol Mirror. Sir, —Having accidentally taken up an old paper of yours (October 20ᵗʰ, 1849), I found it stated, in a very interesting account of the Duke *and* Duchess *privateers, that my grandfather, Alderman Harford, "was the first person who proved that De Foe composed 'Robinson Crusoe', from papers given him by Alexander Selkirk, and that you would be glad of any further information on the subject". I have much pleasure in confirming the account there given, having often heard my father say, "that an old lady (Mrs. Daniel, a daughter of the celebrated Major Wade) told my grandfather that Selkirk had informed her that he had placed his papers in De Foe's hands." My grandfather purchased many of the things which were sold on the return of the* Duke *and* Duchess, *with the rich prize of the Manilla ship, (mentioned by Woodes Rogers, in his account of the voyage, in which Selkirk was found, on the island of Juan Fernandez); they are now in my possession, and consist principally of very handsome china, which was going to the Queen of Spain, with curious articles, in tortoise shell and Indian ink. Captain Rogers . . . lived at Frenchay, in the house now the residence of Mrs. Brice. . . . I am, Sir, your obedient servant, Henry Charles Harford, Brighton, Feb. 26, 1851.*[1]

---

1. R. L. Mégroz, *The Real Robinson Crusoe* (London: The Cresset Press, 1939), pp. 237–38.

After the publication of this letter, a flood of related anecdotes and testimonials appeared in various newspapers, magazines, and academic journals. Pieced together, the story goes as follows.

Nathaniel Wade, town clerk of Bristol, was an old friend of Captain Woodes Rogers, a former Bristol resident. At age twenty, Wade's daughter Damaris married successful merchant John Coysgarne and later made the acquaintance of Daniel Defoe. In 1711 Selkirk returned to England, and in 1713 he visited Bristol. Captain Rogers supposedly introduced Selkirk to Mrs. Coysgarne, who was then living in St. James Square, and she in turn is said to have introduced him to Defoe. At that meeting, Selkirk supposedly handed Defoe the diary he kept on the island, which thus became the basis for Defoe's masterpiece.

Damaris remarried twice during her life, her subsequent surnames being Beck and Daniel. Apparently— this gets complicated—her second husband's first wife was a Harford, and she had a relative named Alderman Harford who actually heard Damaris say that Selkirk himself told her that "he had placed his papers in De Foe's hands." As described in the letter above, that man's grandson Henry Childs Harford remembered this incident, and the letter he wrote to the editor gave credibility to what had formerly been mere rumor.

Yet not a shred of evidence has existed to back up the legend, which was dismissed until recently as far-fetched. But what if there really *was* a diary, after all? Perhaps the petition that had turned up in the papers of the Duke of Hamilton would prove to be the needed "missing link" in the story of the diary and the meeting between the two men.

And what was the "diary" that Selkirk's collateral descendant apparently had? Unfortunately, I never received any reply to my letter. Still, I was unwilling to let
my investigation drop unfinished. On April 25, 1998, I
boarded British Airways Flight 008 for London. Would
Selkirk's descendant show me the diary? Would she
even meet with me? I had no idea, but I wouldn't give
up without a try.

Scotland in late April was chilly. The rain, continual as a
baby's fretful crying, was cold to the touch, and my breath
emerged in white clouds. Still, the bright masses of yellow
heather were a striking sign of spring. I gazed at the rain-
drenched flowers all the way to the village of Largo in the
County of Fife.

How many years had it been since my last visit? Arriving
at the Crusoe Hotel, I felt a rush of nostalgia. Groping my
way there on that long-ago night, confused and anxious, I
had taken the very first steps on this journey without end.

The next morning, I received a phone call from David
Caldwell of the National Museums of Scotland, precisely
at the scheduled time. I had asked him to mediate the
meeting with Selkirk's descendant. Also, in case I was able
to borrow the diary, I needed his professional opinion of
its authenticity.

I listened as Dr. Caldwell spoke, but there was something different about his voice, I thought. He was stum-
bling over his words, unable to conceal his agitation. "I really, just have no idea, what it could mean. . . . You see,
what I mean to say is, she says she doesn't have it any
more!"

Shock left me speechless.

"She says she put it up for auction with Christie's two months ago, and sold it."

As I learned later, the descendant had first acquired the supposed diary on April 29, 1981, at a Christie's auction. She had kept it for seventeen years before suddenly deciding to let it go again. And once again, just as she had done with Selkirk's musket, she gave the item to Christie's for auction.

I confirmed the details of the transaction with Christie's over the telephone. The manuscript had gone on the block March 27, 1998, and was sold to a male bidder living on Jermyn Street in London. No, unfortunately they did not have his telephone number, but they did give me his name.

I set straight to work writing the lucky bidder a letter and sent it off via express mail from the tiny local post office. I wasn't planning to go back to London for a couple of days, and I felt sure that if I sent the new owner of the diary word by special delivery, he'd get it sometime the following day. If all went well, I might hear from him while I was still in Scotland so, just in case, I also wrote where I would be staying in London. I stressed how eager I was to see the diary and how far I had traveled just to do so.

And yet there was of course no guarantee that he would open the letter the following day and immediately send word to me at the Crusoe Hotel: he could have gone away; even worse, he could have already disposed of the diary. There was nothing I could do, but wait . . .

The scene shifts to London. When I checked in at my usual hotel in Soho, a fax message was there waiting for me. It was from the man who had placed the winning bid for the diary. Luck would have it that the fax was extremely faint and hard to read; I pored over it, straining to make out what it said. In the letterhead, alongside his name, address, and telephone number were the words "Antiquarian Books & Manuscripts." So he was a dealer in antique books. The letter continued as follows.

Dear Mr. Takahashi:

Thank you for your letter. I am sorry not to have replied sooner. Yes, I do still have the manuscript here, but I have sold it to a university library in the USA. I am sure you will be allowed to see it, but of course any permission to quote from the manuscript must be arranged with them.

I would be more than happy to show you the manuscript. Please telephone me beforehand to arrange a time, as I am often out.

Yours sincerely,

He'd sold it to a library in the United States? All energy drained out of me, and I slumped glumly to the floor of my hotel room. The letters "USA" loomed up from the letter with heavy finality.

I recalled a similar episode having occurred with Selkirk's musket. As I described in a previous chapter, on learning that the musket had been put up for auction in Edinburgh, Selkirk's relatives had raced to the auction site to buy it back only for their train to be unluckily delayed. In the end, the prize had gone to an American. After the original musket traveled to the

United States, what became of it was unclear, and in the end three different muskets lay claim to being the real one.

I went to see the former owner of the diary at the appointed time. When I entered his office on Jermyn Street, I found the dim interior piled with stacks of leather-bound books. He appeared to be in his late thirties, with a youthful liveliness one doesn't often see among antiquarians. That was my first impression as he entered the room, carrying the precious manuscript.

Emotionally, I explained the history of my interest in the diary, finishing by saying, "I've chased it and chased it, and now, I've finally caught up with it." And then I took it in my hands.

The binding was a leather folder with the words "Memoirs of Alexander Selkirk" stamped in gold on the cover. The gold foil had largely come off, and the worn leather had a soft sheen. Opening the folder, inside I found a manuscript written in black ink on loosely stitched thick paper, with the top sheets detached. The paper, eighty-four sheets in all, was about half the size of ordinary typing paper, and the last seven pages were blank. The manuscript showed signs of corrections and revisions. Entire paragraphs had been crossed out or inserted.

Could this really be Selkirk's journal?

There were no dates on any of the entries. I could see at a glance that it was not what I had been hoping for. This was not the journal alluded to in the old papers of the Duke of Hamilton, which supposedly contained accounts of Selkirk's voyage with Dampier, his life on the island, and his repatriation on the *Duke*.

If it wasn't that, then what was it?

"Memoirs of Alexander Selkirk 11ᵗʰ January 1765." The year 1765 was forty-four years after Selkirk's death. If someone had written it out of sincere motives as a sort of remembrance of Selkirk, the inconsistencies in form and date might be largely accounted for. But to judge whether the author had ever sat down and talked to Selkirk, or known him well, I would have to read it closely and compare its account with the historical record.

Unfortunately, I was unable to read the entire manuscript carefully in my allotted hour. All I could do was establish that this was not, after all, the diary I had anticipated. And in a few days this manuscript would be on its way across the Atlantic to the United States.

I left the man's office on Jermyn Street and walked to the subway station of Green Park; from there, I took the Victoria Line to Vauxhall. Map in hand, I searched for the address I'd been given, and finally arrived at Christie's Firearms Division. It was located in a surprisingly drab building on Ponton Road, and was a part of Christie's vast storage facility. I couldn't help marveling at the scale of the industry to which the cultural institution of the English auction has given rise.

At the reception desk inside I stated my business, and a man soon appeared carrying a large antique gun. "This is the musket given to us by Selkirk's descendants in Scotland," he said. "He wanted it put up for auction, but after examining it we concluded it couldn't possibly be genuine."

In this man's opinion (he was in charge of ancient weapons) the musket was entirely of nineteenth-century English origin. The name "SELKIRK," carved in large letters on one side of the butt, and the year "1705," similarly carved on the other, he pronounced later additions. Having been declared a fake, the musket was no longer suitable for auction and would be returned in due course to its owner.

And so it was settled: this was fake, and the whereabouts of the original musket were unknown. Whether Selkirk's or not, the musket felt heavy and solid in my hands.

I learned through my search for Selkirk's musket and diary that other items belonging to him come up for auction relatively frequently and become the focus of national attention. These include the Bible that was Selkirk's refuge on the island, his inkpot, the cradle he slept in as a newborn baby, and other items. I came away with the strong sense that even in this modern age, Selkirk's memory is very much alive.

I returned to central London and visited a shop on Bond Street specializing in old maps. I told the shop owner that I was looking for a map of Bristol from the 1700s.

Ascertaining whether Selkirk and Defoe had ever met was now all but impossible. Nevertheless, as I pored over the old accounts, I soon realized that Bristol was the only place cited as the probable location of their meeting. There were two possible Bristol addresses: 19 Queens Square, and 16 St. James Square. I wanted to come as close as I could to the facts behind the legend, but a modern map of the city was no help in deciding between the two locales. There were several places called Queens Square, and none called St. James Square. What part of Bristol today would those addresses correspond to? The only way to be sure was to refer to a map of the city as it was in the 1700s.

The oldest map in the shop's enormous folder was made in 1880. I looked up Queens Square and St. James Square in the tiny index in the margin and found one of each, both located in the center of town. I bought the map, went back to my hotel, and set about making a detailed comparison between it and the modern map of Bristol.

The only way to orient myself in looking at the two maps separated by some hundred years was to focus on the River Avon running through the heart of town. In comparison with the Bristol of a century ago, today a complex web of streets surrounded the river, and many of the old street names were gone. Encircling the city was a thick black line representing the beltway around the midtown area. The sight of it filled my mind's eye with visions of bustling traffic.

I stayed up late that night studying the two maps, wondering just how much of present-day Bristol I could explore using a hundred-year-old map. Before long I was aching to get up and go.

The next morning, as soon as I arose I went to Paddington Station and hopped on a train for Bristol. When I got there and began walking around, it seemed to me that the city was new. Yes, the church of Saint Mary Redcliff with its soaring spire had been constructed way back in the fourteenth century as a place to pray for the safety of sailors at sea—but it and the few other reminders of the past were sporadic sights among the newly paved streets and crowded buildings of the downtown area. The impossibility of getting a sense of the past anymore filled me with disappointment. At the same time, it gave me an idea of just what a progressive place this modern Bristol was.

Of the two addresses touted as possible sites for a Defoe-Selkirk meeting, both were connected to Damaris Coysgarne (née Wade), the woman who supposedly brought them together. I decided to look for "19 Queens Square" first.

I was encouraged to see that the stone houses surrounding the square had a vaguely old-fashioned air. With a sidelong glance at boys playing cricket on the lawn, I hunted for number 19. Strangely enough, it wasn't there: the numbers jumped from 18 to 21.

No. 21 was a trim red-brick building with a sign reading "Queens Square House." Just as I was walking past, an old man came out. I quickly collared him and asked him about Damaris Wade. He told me he recalled hearing that before the current house was built in the 1800s, the place had belonged to the Wade family. The fragments of history lingering in his memory were enough to let me know that Damaris Wade could have once lived there.

Next I set out to find "16 St. James Square." Unfortunately, on the spot where my maps told me it should be, the beltway now stood; what it might have looked like long ago was anyone's guess. The old St. James Square had vanished.

However, while examining the street signs in the rotary I made a small discovery: the area is now called "St. James Burton." What was the meaning of the "Burton"? I found in the dictionary that in an old dialect the word meant "the courtyard of a farmhouse." The area had been farmland once; the courtyard surrounded by farm buildings must have become a public square in the 1700s. Today, however, St. James Burton offers nothing to look at but the fierce rush of traffic in both directions.

As evening came, I left Bristol and returned to London. I bought a couple of cold pints of lager from the girl selling them on the train and took my seat. The sun was just setting. A deep crimson flush spread at the horizon, which went on as far as I could see.

As I gazed out on the gathering dusk, I took out a small volume of poetry from my briefcase. The essence of Alexander Selkirk's castaway experience, his sorrow, and the humanity he finally achieved after confronting himself were all fully expressed in a single poem. The poet, William Cowper, lived in the latter half of the eighteenth century and is best known for his long discursive poem "The Task." His poem on Selkirk was published in 1782 as "Verses, Supposed to Be Written by Alexander Selkirk, During His Solitary Abode in the Island of Juan Fernandez."

I am monarch of all I survey,
My right there is none to dispute,
From the centre all round to the sea,
I am lord of the fowl and the brute.
Oh, solitude! where are the charms
That sages have seen in thy face?
Better dwell in the midst of alarms,
Than reign in this horrible place.

I am out of humanity's reach,
I must finish my journey alone,
Never hear the sweet music of speech,
I start at the sound of my own.
The beasts, that roam over the plain,

My form with indifference see;
They are so unacquainted with man,
Their tameness is shocking to me.

Society, friendship, and love,
Divinely bestow'd upon man,
Oh, had I the wings of a dove,
How soon would I taste you again!
My sorrows I then might assuage
In the ways of religion and truth,
Might learn from the wisdom of age,
And be cheer'd by the sallies of youth.

Religion! what treasure untold
Resides in that heavenly word!
More precious than silver and gold,
Or all that this earth can afford.
But the sound of the church-going bell
These vallies and rocks never heard,
Ne're sigh'd at the sound of a knell,
Or smil'd when a sabbath appear'd.

Ye winds, that have made me your sport,
Convey to this desolate shore
Some cordial endearing report
Of a land I shall visit no more.
My friends, do they now and then send
A wish or a thought after me?
O tell me I yet have a friend,
Though a friend I am never to see.

How fleet is a glance of the mind!
Compar'd with the speed of its flight,

The tempest itself lags behind,
And the swift wing'd arrows of light.
When I think of my own native land,
In a moment I seem to be there;
But alas! recollection at hand
Soon hurries me back to despair.

But the sea-fowl is gone to her nest,
The beast is laid down in his lair,
Ev'n here is a season of rest,
And I to my cabin repair.
There is mercy in ev'ry place;
And mercy, encouraging thought!
Gives even affliction a grace,
And reconciles man to his lot.

After reading the poem, I unlaced my dusty shoes and took a nap. When I closed my eyes, I saw again the shore of that island I had once visited. The wind brushed against my cheek and the sound of the waves filled my ears. In my dream, I was swaying lazily in a hammock. I was very happy.

When I returned to Japan, I quickly wrote a letter to the Kenneth Spencer Research Library of the University of Kansas, which had purchased the "Memoirs of Alexander Selkirk," and expressed my desire to spend time going over the diary in detail. They responded by photographing the entire ninety-page manuscript and sending me a copy of it on microfilm. I in turn sent it to Dr. Caldwell in Scotland, asking for his expert opinion.

It turned out not to be Selkirk's journal, after all. Dr. Caldwell's letter shed considerable light on the old document.

28 August 1998

Dear Daisuke

I have read 'Alexander Selkirk's Diary.' It obviously makes several statements which cannot be true, for instance, that Selkirk was brought up in Berwick, that he was still alive in 1765, and that oranges and limes grew on Juan Fernandez. There is other information which cannot be verified, or for which there is no basis—eg that Selkirk first went to sea as a sailor on a ship (a man of war) bound for the Levant (the east end of the Mediterranean, then part of the Turkish Empire).

It is allegedly his memoirs, as written down from 11 January 1765, and it is possible that that is the date of this manuscript. There is the draft of a letter at the back of the volume, dated 16 February 1765, to a lady named Frost, and as far as I am aware, the writing is consistent with that date.

The manuscript is unfinished. It ends with Selkirk being rescued from the island, but there are some scribbled notes which indicate how it was to be completed, with Selkirk returning to London, being dismayed with the wickedness of life there, and returning (or, at least, intending to return) to the island with a select group of friends.

This manuscript, which appears to have been intended for publication, is essentially a moral or religious tale. It is thus in the same tradition as Robinson Crusoe. It has Selkirk sailing from Portsmouth on a ship bound for the South Seas. He takes ill and is put ashore on Juan Fernandez to help him recover. He is accidentally abandoned when his ship sails off to avoid capture by pirates.

Selkirk discovers that the island offers all that is necessary for a comfortable life. His only major regret is the lack of companionship from other humans. But he realizes that he owes everything to a benign God who is watching over him.

This manuscript demonstrates the continuing interest in the 18th century in 'getting back to nature' and avoiding the wickedness and complexity of (Western/European) society and culture.

I believe its main importance to you is how Selkirk's experience as a castaway continued to catch the imagination.

I hope this will be of some use to you. I am glad to have had the opportunity to see the diary. I will keep the copy and film of the manuscript until I hear from you—in case I have to refer to them again. Write and let me know if I can do anything else.
All best wishes,
David Caldwell

The legend remained just that—a legend.

CHAPTER

Eight

Discovery

The man gave me a long look, then turned and plunged into the brush. Soon he was gone from sight. I could hear rustling, and exclamations of pain. I prepared to follow him. The dense tangle of sharp-thorned blackberry brambles was daunting, but now there was a small opening. I got down on all fours and crawled in. Hard, needle-like thorns jabbed and tore at me from all sides, easily penetrating my heavy long-sleeved shirt. I squirmed and inched my way along, painfully. The thorns were everywhere: on top of me, before me, behind me, to my right, to my left—even on the ground, driving up into my kneecaps as I crept on.

Looking ahead, I was able to see the man's slow advance by the fluctuations of his shadow. In his hand was a well-used bush knife that attacked the brambles with each swing of his arm, but never with the satisfying *thwack* of a clean slice.

My own progress was far from swift. The walls of bramble pressed against me, holding me back, shutting me in. I struggled desperately, beating my way through with a short stick.

Time went by, and the farther we made our way in, the heavier, thicker, and denser the woods became. It seemed impenetrable. And yet, this was once a pathway known as "Pioneer Trail." Traces of an old animal trail were barely visible in the ground. The origin of the path was indeed ancient; the villagers claimed it predated the arrival of colonists in the mid-eighteenth century. And the man I was following claimed to have seen something at the end of the trail, forty years ago.

Now here was I, going down that very Pioneer Trail under his guidance. The torturous struggle with the overgrown blackberry brambles took me to the very edge of exhaustion. Then I saw it.

The shock was stupendous. Time seemed to stand still.

January 31, 2001: that was the day I finally found what I'd been looking for on Robinson Crusoe Island.

To explain, I must go further back, to October 1999—the day I visited Dr. David Caldwell at the National Museums of Scotland. False leads concerning Alexander Selkirk's reputed diary had sent me chasing up and down the United Kingdom, with little or nothing to show for my efforts. In fact, all my research had reached a dead end. I had uncovered nothing conclusive about a meeting between Defoe and Selkirk. Nor had I made any new discovery on Robinson Crusoe Island.

I still had a chance, though, I thought. I knew I was being an optimist, but I was not in any mood to call it quits.

In the meantime, Dr. Caldwell graciously invited me on an archaeological project. The prospect fascinated me. Close inspection of a set of NASA radar images taken in 1990 by the space shuttle had revealed the existence of apparent Viking ruins buried on the Scottish island of Islay. It seemed that Vikings had gone to the island to mine its lead deposits and had founded a settlement there. The site was unexcavated, but radar images clearly showed the disposition of buried houses and roads. Dr. Caldwell and his two colleagues were creating a database of every historical building and site on the island, a slow and painstaking process. I stood with them in the level areas between mounds, picturing the buried roads and trying to imagine the lives of the people who had trodden them long ago. It was an exciting moment, and it eventually provided the clue that brought my own research out of the doldrums.

Remote sensing based on radar images, used mainly for weather monitoring and observations to protect the earth's environment, is increasingly being applied as an aid to archaeological discovery, I learned. The ability of long-wavelength microwaves to penetrate the earth's surface to a depth of ten feet or more, especially in dry, sandy areas, has enabled scientists to pinpoint the location of many an ancient ruin and riverbed. Moreover, NASA space shuttle missions have completed radar observations of virtually every inch of the earth's surface. The obvious question occurred to me: why wouldn't radar observation data collected over the Juan Fernandez Archipelago reveal the long-lost site of Alexander Selkirk's shelter?

I managed to e-mail a contact at NASA headquarters in Pasadena, California. They were intrigued by my quest for "Robinson Crusoe's house" and agreed to help. Unfortunately, the Juan Fernandez Islands had not been included in the 1990 space shuttle survey. I tried to find other satellite radar surveys, and even sent an inquiry to United States Geological Survey, but in the end it became clear that, for my particular search, remote sensing was of little value. For one thing, the only buried ruins it would expose would be those showing up as lines (rivers and roads) or planes (large temples from ancient civilizations)—whereas Alexander Selkirk's huts, seen from outer space, would be no more than tiny pinpricks. Besides, the area to be surveyed would have to be free of vegetation, but I knew from my own explorations that whatever might be left of the huts would lie deep in the mountains, overgrown with trees and grass. And so, to my great regret, I had to rule out remote sensing as a way of pinpointing the location of the elusive remains. Yet the time I'd spent on this endeavor was not wasted: this detour helped awaken me to an important fact that I'd been overlooking.

One day as I was exchanging views with Dr. Caldwell, he made the following casual remark: "If you could obtain radar images, they probably would show the stone walls . . ."

I almost let it slide, but somehow the word "stone" alerted me. "Why stone?" I protested mildly. "Nothing in the literature says he built his house out of stone."

Woodes Rogers, the man who rescued Selkirk from years of isolation, described the huts as being made of pimento wood, long grasses, and goatskin. Not a word about stone. In that sense I was right—but I was like the student who learns the textbook by rote without giving it deep thought. Dr. Caldwell's explanation of his theory soon made me realize the narrowness of my approach.

"Selkirk's being Scottish has great significance when you try to guess what sort of shelter he built for himself," he pointed out. "The cold climate and strong winds of Scotland make it unsuitable for trees big enough to use in construction. That's why you find almost all houses in Scotland are made of stone—unlike in England, where they tend to be made of brick. The use of stone is part of Scottish culture, tied to the natural environment. If someone born and bred in Scotland was forced to live on a desert island and build a house, what could be more natural than to use stone?"

Until then, I'd treated my written sources as sacred texts, accepting them with a kind of blind faith. In the contemplation of history, written records are of course an invaluable source of information—yet no record is ever complete. The data are fragmentary. Attempting to deduce the nature of Selkirk's huts solely from the literature, without taking into account the man's own background, was possibly misleading.

What were houses in eighteenth-century Scotland actually like? To find out, I tramped all over Scotland in the company of Dr. Caldwell. In County Fife in the Lowlands we saw the lovely town of Culross, which looks the same today as when it was built in Selkirk's time, its stone houses and cobbled roads typifying the medieval Scottish town. We went to the Highlands, where again, even around Loch Ness of water-monster fame, the houses were made of stone. Finally we reached scenic western

Scotland, where a chain of picturesque islands lies in an arc off the Atlantic coast. Carefully preserved on the island of Lewis in the Outer Hebrides—an island chain whose very name means "farthest end"—was a traditional stone house called "Black House." It had mortared walls made with round, uncut stones, and an earthen roof built on a foundation of wood, slate, and grass. The primitive look of the rounded dirt roof and stone walls strongly conveyed what Scottish residences must have been like in previous centuries.

"Do you suppose Selkirk's hut was something like this?" I asked Dr. Caldwell.

"Yes, I think this probably gives a very good idea," he answered thoughtfully, holding out his hands to the fragrant white peat smoke from the fireplace in Black House.

After returning to London, I hurried to the British Library on Euston Road, where I was to spend many days. I felt compelled to go back and carefully reread every source I could think of: material on Selkirk, records of his passage to Juan Fernandez Island, old maps of the island, books on local plant and animal life. These materials had provided the basis for my search, yet I had mainly relied mostly on legwork. Now, after learning about satellite radar surveys and spending time with Dr. Caldwell, I was ready to go back and pore over these sources. Undoubtedly they contained points I'd inadvertently missed. And indeed, after days in the British Library, I felt the scales fall from my eyes.

Keeping in mind my personal knowledge of the island, I returned once again to Woodes Rogers's account of his rescue of Selkirk, and I now saw for the first time that it contained distinct clues to the area where Selkirk had lived. The description was so simple and clear that I was astounded to think I could have overlooked it all this time.

> *Febr. 11. Yesterday in the Evening having little or nothing to do with the Pinnace, we sent her to the South End of the Island to get Goats. The Governour told us, that during his stay he could not get down to that end from the Mountains where he liv'd, they were so steep and rocky; but that there were abundance of Goats there, and that part of the Island was plainer. Capt. Dampier, Mr Glendal, and the Governour, with ten Men, set out in company with the Dutchess's Boat and Crew, and surrounded a great parcel of Goats, which are of a larger sort, and not so wild as those on the higher part of the Island where the Governour liv'd; but not looking well to 'em, they escap'd over the Cliff.*[1]

What mountains were these? According to Rogers's account, this was where Selkirk had made his home. Apparently unable to descend the mountains to the south, he could still look out in that direction and so knew there were lots of goats. He had to have lived on the northern side of the mountains, at a high elevation. That was where the huts had been.

Instinctively I recalled something Mauricio Calderon of CONAF had told me the last time I visited the island. He'd said that while there was now a path leading south from Selkirk's Lookout (El Mirador) to the Villagra district, in Selkirk's time it would have been too steep to be passable. And as the record clearly indicates, the area

---

1. Woodes Rogers, *A Cruising Voyage round the World* (London: Bell and B. Lintot, 1712), pp. 123–37.

south of the cliffs, including the Villagra district, is level.

Then in the map room, I found something intriguing. On a 1680 copy by William Hack of an English-language map of Juan Fernandez Island by Basil Ringrose, the area from the present Villagra district to the southwest end of the island was labeled "Goat Quarter." That established that the area to the south that Selkirk used to look down upon, where so many goats lived, included Villagra and all the land beyond to the southwest.

Where could one have looked down on the "Goat Quarter?" The answer was clear: Selkirk's Lookout. My own trekking had also established that that was the sole place on the island with a good view of Villagra that also enjoyed easy access to and from the bottom of the northern slope.

Another old map showed the lay of the land around Selkirk's Lookout and Cumberland to the north. Included in the log of Captain George Anson, who visited the island in 1741, the map plainly showed a path between Cumberland Bay and El Mirador, as well as a number of paths in Cumberland connecting to the rivers and forests.

My own explorations, the data I had gathered, and my rereading of the literature together spelled out where Selkirk's huts had been. Selkirk had lived north of his lookout, in Cumberland (my Zone C).

> *He built two Hutts with Pimento Trees, cover'd them with long Grass, and lin'd them with the Skins of Goats. . . . In the lesser Hutt, at some distance from the other, he dress'd his Victuals, and in the larger he slept, and employ'd himself in reading, singing Psalms, and praying.*[2]

2. Rogers, *A Cruising Voyage round the World*, pp. 123–27.

Assuming Dr. Caldwell was correct in his surmise that the huts were built partly of stone, what was the "long grass" mentioned here? Carl Skottsberg's definitive study of the island's natural history, *The Natural History of Juan Fernandez and Easter Islands,* vol. 2, *Botany,* listed several possible candidates, and the likelihood of getting any more specific information seemed nil. Yet when I contacted CONAF official Mauricio Calderon again, he told me that his studies suggested the long grass was a member of the family *Gramineae.* Going back to Skottsberg's book, I found that that plant had existed all over the island.

Since I had already ascertained that the pimento wood mentioned in the passage was actually luma wood, it became evident that the building materials for his huts—including goatskin—were available everywhere on the island. Therefore, pinpointing the geographic location of the huts on the basis of those materials alone was impossible.

The relative locations of the two huts should be calculable based on their use. The larger of the two was used as a living room and would of course have been at a higher elevation with a good view of Cumberland Bay; the other, a smaller area used as a combination kitchen and dining room, would have been in a level place along a stream nearer to the bay. And both of them would have been built in inconspicuous spots, to guard against intrusions by hostile Spaniards.

One after another, facts I had not gleaned in my previous readings became clear. I felt the old dream of finding the remains of the huts reawaken within me.

But my own investigation of Cumberland in 1994 had made me painfully aware that the chance of finding any ruins there was slim. People had settled there, developing the land until any prospect of a special discovery seemed hopelessly remote. Close reading of the historical writings of my predecessors, too, made me certain that no centuries-old ruins could possibly remain.

Some forty years after Selkirk's departure, Spanish colonists came to the island and founded the village of San Juan Bautista on the flat land near Cumberland Bay. Records indicate that 255 people came over, including 62 soldiers, 171 volunteer colonists, and 22 criminals. They encountered an unforeseen trial.

> *On the night of May 25, 1751 . . . a terrible earthquake completely destroyed the works. The devastating tidal wave that followed wreaked terror and ruin on the island, as well as at Concepción and Valparaíso. The tremor shook the new structures down or loosened them and the mighty wave finished the job, destroying completely the houses and the fort and drowning at least 38 of the inhabitants who had not gained higher ground. Colonel Navarro, along with all of his family and servants were among those lost. Sobrecasas survived because he had bult his hut on higher ground, as had many of the other settlers. Terror and panic ruled the island following the tidal wave as the inhabitants, many of them scantily clad, fled to the hills.*[3]

The damage from this earthquake and tsunami forced the colonists to rebuild their lives from scratch. Many took the opportunity to return to the Chilean mainland. At the same time, relief shipments arrived from Chile, and the rebuilding of the village began.

---

3. Ralph Lee Woodward, Jr., *Robinson Crusoe's Island: A History of the Juan Fernández Islands* (Chapel Hill: University of North Carolina Press, 1969), p. 84.

Most of the armaments and fortifications had been carried away.
The houses on the lowland along the shore had disappeared. They
built the new fort on the bluff overlooking the town, and several
houses sprung up on the hillside as well.[4]

As the above passage indicates, people learned their lesson after the earthquake and tsunami and avoided rebuilding along the shore, choosing a higher elevation instead. This historical fact proved fatal to the attempt to
discover the remains of Selkirk's huts.

No small hut such as would have existed near the shore
along the lower reaches of the river could possibly have
escaped the effects of the tsunami. Even if by some miracle it had, there was other evidence to suggest that any
trace of the houses had been destroyed. Maria Graham
visited the island in 1823 and left this account of abandoned houses she found:

A few houses and cottages are still in tolerable condition, though
most of the doors, windows, and roofs have been taken away, or
used as fuel by whalers and other ships touching here.[5]

Most of the subsequent visitors to the island looked on
remnants of previous residents' lives as resources on
which they could draw to build their own lives. It is not
hard to imagine from Graham's account that the pimento
wood used by Selkirk in constructing his house was glee-
fully appropriated as firewood.

---

4. Woodward, *Robinson Crusoe's Island*, p. 84.

5. Maria Graham, *A Journal of a Residence in Chile, and a Voyage from
Chile to Brazil in the year 1822–3*, 25th January 1823, in John Howell's
The Life and Adventures of Alexander Selkirk (London: Oliver & Boyd,
1829), p. 160.

She also went to a cavern in Cumberland, where she was moved to write pityingly as follows:

After dinner we went to the western side of the town, and there ad-mired the extraordinary regularity of the structure of the rocks, and some curious caverns like those of Monte Albano. In one of the largest of these we found an enormous goat dead, which of course reminded us of "Poor Robin Crusoe."[6]

The cavern she refers to, later known as Patriots' Cave, is one that deportees began inhabiting from 1814. In her knowledge of Selkirk, Maria Graham here becomes the first recorded visitor to the island to be aware that he was the model for Robinson Crusoe. She was in that sense the very first tourist to Robinson Crusoe Island.

From a historiographic perspective, this awareness marks an important turning point. Until his link with Crusoe gave him some universal standing, Selkirk was just another English pirate, relics of whose residence drew no special attention. That is precisely what makes Graham's account so valuable. From this point on, any discoveries pertaining to Selkirk's life on the island, real or imagined, would be respectfully preserved.

Unfortunately, Graham makes no direct comments about Selkirk's residence. Were the huts already gone by the time of her visit?

I continued to trace the documentary record, coming next to the account of an American named E. I. Barra who visited the island twenty-six years later, in 1849. Here I came across a clear reference to the place where Selkirk lived.

---

6. Graham, *A Journal of a Residence in Chile*, p. 165.

As Governor Echandea had told us that the cave of Robinson Crusoe was about one and a half miles to the westward, in a small cove that could be easily reached by a boat, but would take a day to go by land, we asked the mate for permission to use one of the boats for the purpose. We accordingly took the boat, and four of us rowed around the promontory into the cove of which I had read so much in the delightful story of Robinson Crusoe. The little cove is a repetition of the one where the ship was laying, but very diminutive in size. The cave was a few rods from the margin of the sea, on an elevation opening towards the sea, and from which the recluse had a full view, and a visual sweep of the ocean.

It was here that the poor shipwrecked mariner passed four lonely years of his adventurous life. It was here that he trained his goats, watched the seafowls and the wild beast that roamed around on the precipitous cliffs. It was on this very spot that he had cultivated his little garden. The poor fellow! I could almost picture him as standing before me, with his unique garments of goat skins, looking, with longing eyes, out upon the broad expanse of ocean to, perchance, discover some friendly sail, that might be directed hitherward by a kind Providence, to rescue the poor shipwrecked mariner.[7]

By this time, people were making the unequivocal assumption that the little cave in Puerto Inglés (Robinson Crusoe's Cave) was where Selkirk had lived. Generations of islanders told visitors again and again that that was where Selkirk spent the four years and four months of his exile. In time it became such an accepted "historical fact" that a marker was erected.

---

7. E. I. Barra, *A Tale of Two Oceans: New Story by Old Californian, An Account of a Voyage from Philadelphia to San Francisco, Around Cape Horn. Years 1849–50, calling at Rio de Janeiro, Brazil, and at Juan Fernandez, in the South Pacific*, San Francisco, 1893, pp. 173–74.

My perusal of the sources gave me a graphic lesson in the origins of history. All the more reason why I had to set off once again for the island, to find some trace of Alexander Selkirk's huts in Cumberland.

At the start of my journey, I received interesting news of a treasure hunt in progress on the island. The October 2000 edition of the Spanish magazine *Muy Interesante* gave details. To sum up, the treasure hunt was touched off by an old sheepskin letter that the proprietress of an island inn had inherited from her stepfather. Written in the late 1700s by a British naval officer named Webb, the letter was addressed to a Captain George Anson but had apparently turned up in South America, undelivered. Its contents alluded to the existence of treasure on the island.

An intrigued American conducted a follow-up search in England, where he succeeded in locating two other letters mailed by Webb to Anson from South America. Together, the three Webb letters made it possible to form a hazy conjecture regarding the site of the trove. This in turn naturally sparked off a full-blown excavation by Chilean authorities.

The treasure being sought on Robinson Crusoe Island was said to be part of unpaid tribute owed to Spain by eighteenth-century aristocrats in Peru. After learning of its existence while crossing the South Sea, Captain George Anson later enlisted Webb to go under cover of secrecy and retrieve it for him. But when the other seamen found out about his secret mission, they plotted to kill him and take the treasure for themselves. Webb sensed which way the wind was blowing and took swift action, setting fire to the ship and fleeing in a rowboat. He made it as far as South America, but was unlucky: he contracted malaria there and died before he could return home. He did, though, manage to write to Anson three times about the elusive treasure. Of the three missives, two were safely delivered to the addressee—but by then Anson himself was also dead.

The excavation began in earnest in November 1999. The site of the dig was none other than "Robinson Crusoe's Cave" in Puerto Inglés, and its vicinity.

In January 2001, I arrived back on the island. In six years, nothing had changed. The smiles of fishermen being rocked in their boats, the wind, the waves, the smell of the ocean, the slow flow of time—everything was just as I remembered it. I felt a rush of nostalgia for the shape of the mountains, the rivers and streams, the wharf of the fishing village San Juan Bautista, and its Main Street and houses. My ears were filled with the sound of waves. "I'm back!" I yelled. It seemed to me that everyone was smiling.

But I was unable to see any faces I recognized or meet with any of the people I remembered so well. The old Frenchman hadn't been seen around the island for some years, I was told, and the boys I'd gotten to know had all left for the mainland too.

Robinson Crusoe's Cave in Puerto Inglés was altered beyond recognition. The back of the cave had been removed to facilitate the excavation, and scaffolding had been erected. Excavated dirt was packed into light red sacks that lay around in piles. In front of the cave were workers' rain gear and tools. This was no casual "treasure hunt" but a genuine archaeological investigation.

"No treasure so far," the villagers informed me, "but they have turned up pieces of some kind of pottery."

For centuries this island lay in the South Seas all but unnoticed, but now, thanks to rumors of buried treasure, it was gaining wider recognition. The lives of the villagers would perhaps never be the same.

Thus it was not a total accident that I met the man.

One of the participants in the Puerto Inglés cave hunt, a fisherman, had dug something up. It was an ordinary piece of unglazed pottery, and he thought nothing of it until the archaeologist in charge explained how valuable a find it really was. A piece of unglazed ware from deep in the earth had much to tell about the unknown past; furthermore, it might very well provide a link to the treasure itself. For the fisherman, the notion that an artifact exhumed from the earth might reveal island history made little sense and held little interest. But if it were true that the dull bit of pottery had some connection to the buried treasure, that was another story. For the next few days, the man eagerly kept on digging.

That's when it happened: a lost boyhood memory came back to him. When he was twelve, he had gone off in pursuit of a runaway cow, following it into the Cumberland mountains. The half-wild cow moved nimbly, and the young boy soon lost sight of her. It had been raining, however, and the marks of her hooves were plain to see in the soft earth. He kept on climbing, following her trail.

After a while he found the cow standing still in a flat area. He crept stealthily through the grass toward her, careful not to attract attention. When he got up close, he saw she was motionless inside an enclosure of some kind. The ground inside the enclosure was hollowed out, with an unglazed pot about twelve inches in diameter lying inside.

The middle-aged man remembered the place from boyhood with crystal clarity. The idea that that pot might be the one with some connection to buried treasure began to consume him. He went off alone into the mountains to look for the enclosure again. And he found it, in an overgrown tangle of blackberry bushes. More than forty years had passed since his first glimpse of the place, but there was no sign of any interim visitors. From then on, that was the man's own secret place.

Even so, he made no attempt to seal it off. "I know where there's something amazing up in the mountains." Everyone on the island had heard his boast. Yet he never took anyone from the village up there. He had another reason to keep it secret: he used wood from those mountains to make his lobster traps. That was his lifeline. He did not want anyone else from the village poking his nose around there.

So far, no one but the man himself knew where it was.

As soon as I caught wind of that mysterious place in Cumberland, I was consumed with the need to see it for myself. The description of the clumsy enclosure where the cow had been found sounded enticingly like what might be left of an old residence.

On January 31, 2001, I went to meet the man. His beard and sharp eyes were striking. He seemed aloof, yet as we began to talk with the help of an interpreter, I soon saw him reveal a frank and openhearted side. When two people don't talk the same language, a man's gestures and expressions speak worlds. We quickly became friends, and I was able to win his trust. He agreed to take me to his secret place—a place that few people on earth have ever visited. I am bound to respect the promise I made him that day, and so I will not reveal here any details about its name or location.

It was in a totally unexpected area. As I followed the man down the mountain, the ridge suddenly leveled out. We kept on going, skirting fallen trees. What surprised me more than anything was that in 1994, I'd traveled up and down that very slope countless times. The area was one I knew well and, amazingly, that stormy night when I put up my tent, enduring the torment of sharp blackberry brambles, I'd been only a stone's throw away.

And the next day, during my struggle to escape the clutches of the blackberries, I'd headed for the stream at the bottom of the mountain. Its murmuring echoed through the trees, a promise of abundant water. But no matter how I tried, I couldn't reach the riverbank, and I ended up going all the way down the slope without ever realizing what had been abandoned farther up.

Thinking back to this, I followed the man. At every step, the sound of crackling twigs and rustling leaves filled the air. There was no other sound—no birdsong, no beating of hummingbird wings. Silence reigned.

Finally my companion came to a halt. He motioned to me and said slowly, "Here. This is it."

I looked and began trembling with excitement. I lost the power of speech. Again and again I walked around, drinking in the scene. Brambles surrounding the site scratched me at every turn, but what did that matter? Look at it! Look! I told myself. An ancient house, half buried in the dirt! A house made of stone.

Finally I was able to take stock of the surroundings. The stone remains formed a rectangle, six meters by four [twenty by thirteen feet]. Just the right size for one person to live comfortably. There was some variation according to the settling of the ground, but the portion showing ranged from twelve to fifteen inches in height. The visible stones, covered here and there with a light coating of moss, were carefully piled up with mortar. Looking closely, I saw signs of other stones lying piled up or side by side on the outside of the wall, too. That might be where the wall had collapsed during the earthquake. Mostly the stones were rounded, with no sharp edges, just like the other stones in the area. Only one showed signs of having been cut in two places in an attempt to level it off.

The mountain behind the stone walls appeared to have been dug up in one place. The soil was clay. Apparently it had been used to make mortar for the walls and pottery.

I paid careful attention to the surrounding vegetation. Most of it was maqui trees and blackberry bushes, which were both introduced to the island after 1960. Moss on the stones must have set in after those nonnative plants grew tall enough to form a canopy giving protection from the sun. Mentally subtracting the nonnative plant species from the scene, I could see that this hill would have been a comfortable place to live, with sunlight filtering pleasantly through the leaves. There was still a scattering of the luma trees that Selkirk had relied on for sustenance; I found the sight of one luma tree sapling growing inside the stone enclosure particularly striking.

"How far is it from here to the nearest fresh water?" I asked suddenly.

"Not far. Just a short walk."

He led me to it. On the way, we came to a ridge with a view of the sea.

"Nice view of Cumberland Bay," I commented.

"Not like what it used to be," he replied. "You could see it better when I was a boy." Back in 1955, when the man first came to this place, blackberries and maqui tree had yet to encroach upon the island. As he grew into adulthood and middle age, the island scenery underwent its own slow transformation.

As we descended the slope, the man pointed to a tiny opening through the blackberry shrubs and told me, "There used to be a path here. Nobody comes this way any more, though."

"Why not?"

"A mudslide wrecked the path. It used to be the only direct route from the bay to El Mirador."

"Is the path today different from the old one?"

"It was made after 1970. I heard my grandfather say when I was a little boy that this other path was formed by pioneers a long, long time ago."

We went back to the stone ruins, and I asked some more questions.

"It looks as though earth has been piled up on top of the stones. Does anyone living on the island have a house built like this?"

"All our houses are made of wood. No one uses stones to build a house."

"Then you must have been surprised the first time you saw this."

"I was just a boy, so I didn't know anything. When I told my father about it, he said it must be the remains of a secret ammunition storehouse for the fort in the foothills, which is still there. It's made of stone, too. At the time, I never questioned the truth of what he said. But the stones in the fort are cut and sanded. It's impossible to think this wall was made by the same technology. It's a more complicated structure than you'd need for a storehouse, and besides, it's too far from the fort for all practical purposes. It must have been something else."

"You said you found a pot here," I went on. "Where is it now?"

"It's gone. I smashed it and threw it away, a long time ago."

"What was it like?"

"Just an ordinary unglazed pot."

"Did it have any design?"

"No, nothing like that."

"Was there anything inside?"

"No, it was empty. Or wait, maybe there was dead leaves and dirt inside."

As he answered my stream of questions, it seemed that the man began to share my enthusiasm. The sun had gone down behind the mountain, and the sea breeze sweeping up from below warmed the chilly slope. The trees swayed and rustled in the wind.

"Who lived here?" I murmured. My companion was silent. I whispered the question again to the stone walls. They, too, were stolid and silent.

And time moved on.

After returning from the island, I pored over my photographs and notes, organizing my information and sketching it out. I factored in the elevation of the primary site, the location of water, and the correlation of each with the old Pioneer Trail; the scale of the ruins; the slope with clay deposits; the position of Selkirk's Lookout relative to the house; the nearby view; and so on. Then I compared my results with the topographical map I'd recently received from Mauricio Calderon of CONAF. He had left his post, but the map was completed during his tenure to aid in preservation of the environment. Then once again I read over my materials on Selkirk and picked up a copy of *Robinson Crusoe*.

Now I knew that what I had found on the island exceeded all my expectations. I sat down and wrote a long letter to my old friend Dr. David Caldwell, summing up my thoughts.

Dear David,

My analysis of the ruins that I've recently discovered leads me to believe they were the peculiar residence of a peculiar individual. Of course, as far as I can tell, in terms of water supply, land, and surrounding environment, the site perfectly satisfies every need for human habitation in the wild, and would have been a comfortable place to live. But in considering the island overall, there's something that's hard for me to understand. The more I turn it over in my mind, the more unnatural it seems, and that's what makes me think there is something fairly peculiar about the place.

If I'd built a house on the island, where would I have put it? Probably in an open space near the shore—yet the ruins lie deep in the mountains, a place where to this day no one ever goes. What accounts for the difference? I can only guess, yet it seems plain enough that whoever lived in that house felt compelled to hide. I can't help thinking that a man's motives and grounds for going to such lengths to avoid being conspicuous, and the state of mind that might compel him to do so, are miles removed from ordinary sensibility. The island is after all an abundant and peaceful place.

Though the site is so densely overgrown that from the bay it is invisible, it affords an excellent view of Cumberland to the north. On the one hand it discourages observation by others; on the other, it commands a fine view of the sea. That's another peculiarity. Whoever lived there had a strong desire to look out onto the ocean.

After accidentally discovering a human footprint along the shore, Robinson was filled with anxiety. To prevent his house overlooking the ocean from being found by enemies, he began carefully planting trees all around it. He then has this to say about his house:

> *Thus in two years time I had a thick grove, and in five or six years time I had a wood before my dwelling, growing so monstrous thick and strong, that it was indeed perfectly impassable; and no men of what kind soever would ever imagine that there was any thing beyond it, much less a habitation.*[8]

When this passage leaped out at me, I felt as if a bright torch had been lit in a dark cavern. The images of two men who'd been completely separate in my mind, the one fiction and the other non-fiction, now fit together smoothly. It was an absolutely perfect match. The master of that stone house, whoever he was, had shared Robinson's mind and experience.

The house belonged to someone who was cast away on a desert island and then hid himself from potential enemies while yet continuing to gaze out to sea, clinging to hope of rescue. It was the house of Robinson Crusoe.

Alexander Selkirk, of course, while living in isolation on the island, was forced to build a hut in a secluded place where hostile Spaniards would not find him. While historically he was not the only person ever obliged to live on the island, I would say that the circumstances he endured of having to dodge enemies while seeking rescue from his isolation were highly peculiar.

Were those ruins actually the site of Selkirk's house? It's certainly tempting to think so. As you once said it would be, the house was made of stone. Your prediction was spot on. The moment I saw the ruins, a voice inside me yelled, "Wow! Fantastic!"

---

8. Daniel Defoe, *Robinson Crusoe,* (New York: Penguin Classics, 1985), p. 169.

It was like being witness to a divine revelation. Without ever hav-
ing gone to the island, you foretold what was there. I went and
saw it with my own eyes—an amazing experience.

But it doesn't pay to be hasty. I have to make an effort to stay
cool and objective.

Since the stone walls are mostly buried underground, it's hard
to say for sure, but they did strike me as very similar to those of
Black House. While looking at the ruins, I thought back to that
ancient Scottish house in the Outer Hebrides we visited together.
The stones were round and uncut, piled with mortar and covered
with earth, exactly as at Black House. Such outer similarity is no
basis for declaring that that was where Selkirk lived; as you
pointed out, it only suggests the possibility that the house was
built by a Scot.

To me, the most direct and compelling link between Selkirk and
the ruins is their location vis-à-vis his lookout. They are nearby.
The old route from Cumberland Bay to Selkirk's Lookout goes
straight past the ruins. Whoever lived there visited the lookout on
a daily basis. That much is beyond dispute. And the only person
who lived alone on the island with Selkirk's Lookout as the cen-
ter of his existence was Alexander Selkirk.

The circumstantial evidence is all there.

Bull's-eye.

Still, the final answer will have to wait for an archeological
survey. And unfortunately, one won't be happening anytime
soon. The entire island is under special protection now as a na-
tional park, for one thing, and for another, the ruins are in an
area of particular importance to the livelihood of fishermen. As
you always say, excavations aren't easy. I'm keenly aware of the
need to proceed with caution to avoid disrupting either the envi-
ronment or the lives of local residents. But among the handful of
visitors to the site is a Chilean archeologist who I'm sure will take
part in a dig there, sooner or later. Even then, nothing definitive
may turn up. There are no acquaintances or contemporaries of
Selkirk around to tell us for sure whether any artifacts there be-
longed to him. Unless something inscribed with his name comes

along, we may never be able to declare with certainty that that was where Selkirk lived.

But no matter what future investigations may or may not bring to light, I am content and thankful that after seven years of searching I was finally able, this time, to find those ruins.

Because I did it. I established something once and for all. I went to Robinson Crusoe Island and found Robinson Crusoe's house.

All the best,
Daisuke Takahashi

Epilogue

Did the Two Men Ever Really Meet?

The letter I received from Dr. Caldwell at the end of summer 1998 put a damper on my investigation of Selkirk's journal. Of course, if the real journal ever turned up, it would be possible to learn more about his daily life on the island and also to verify where he had set up camp and built his huts.

A close examination of the historical record revealed that in 1720, eleven years after Selkirk's repatriation, the English ship *Speedwell* ran aground and broke up in the Juan Fernandez Islands. Forty-seven men escaped with their lives to Mas-a-Tierra, including Captain George Shelvocke. After only five months of castaway life, they managed to build themselves a new ship, which they christened *Recovery*, and sailed off in a dramatic escape.

Captain George Shelvocke published the log of that journey in 1726. Perhaps his account included mention of traces of a predecessor, I thought. The Public Record Office introduced me to Roger Nixon, a professional researcher with expertise in naval history, whom I hired to look into that possibility for me. Unfortunately, he established that nothing in the captain's log had any bearing on Selkirk's experience.

Then what about the 1868 records of the HMS *Topaze?* As I mentioned in chapter three, Commodore Powell and his officers put up a monument to Selkirk at his lookout. I hoped that that ship's log might contain some sort of comment about the huts, but again, I was disappointed. Mr. Nixon found two logs for the *Topaze*, neither of which mentioned anything about the men's doings ashore.

When these investigations were over, I truly felt that I had done all I could. Until some new documentary evidence turned up, the mystery would have to remain a mystery.

Frances Selkirk's petition to the Duke of Hamilton and the legend of a meeting in Bristol between Defoe and Selkirk, during which Selkirk's journal changed hands, were connected only by their intimation that Selkirk had actually kept a diary. There was nothing to do but sit tight and see whether the diary surfaced or whether any other corroborating evidence came along.

Concerning the possibility of a meeting between the two men, however, I felt a careful review of the existing record might yet yield important clues. I proceeded to sift through everything I had learned about Selkirk and apply it to my reading of *Robinson Crusoe,* to see what I might come up with.

After all I had done to piece together Selkirk's life and retrace his actual footsteps, my image of the man whose experiences inspired *Robinson Crusoe* was now a full-bodied one. No superman, he was prone to human failings, from the hotheadedness that got him abandoned on the island in the first place to the impetuosity of writing two "final" wills and testaments in a short space of time that named two different women as beneficiary. And above all, there was the striking contrast between his anguished longing for human contact during his four-year exile, and the world-weariness of his life after being rescued and returned to England. In all of these details that never found their way into the novel, I found compelling evidence of a living, breathing human being.

In the novel, meanwhile, Robinson Crusoe has this to say about his life after settling back in England:

> . . . *first of all I marry'd, and that not either to my disadvantage or dissatisfaction, and had three children, two sons and one daughter: but my wife dying, and my nephew coming home with good success from a voyage to Spain, my inclination to go abroad, and his importunity, prevailed and engaged me to go in his ship, as a private trader to the East Indies.*

This brief summation contains no hint of the suffering Selkirk experienced due to the discrepancy between his idealized longing for human society and the reality he encountered on his return.

For Defoe, accustomed as he was to a journalist's perspective on what society ought to be, the novel was doubtless another means of shedding light on that topic through the life of an individual man. For that reason, it is hard for me to believe that he could have met in person with Selkirk, questioned him about what had gone through his mind on the island and what he thought after returning to human society, and then blithely disregarded all of that information. It seems unlikely that he would have passed over Selkirk's psychological struggles and the contradictions in his nature as thematic material for his novel.

The nature of his relationships with his contemporaries also suggests to me that Defoe had little need to meet with Selkirk in order to write *Robinson Crusoe*. As a journalist, he would no doubt have accepted Captain Woodes Rogers's eyewitness account as ideal documentary evidence. Not only that, Richard Steele, who did in fact meet with Selkirk and write an essay based on that encounter, was Defoe's colleague and rival. To offer a warmed-over version of another man's work would have been cause for shame.

So whether I looked at the matter using inductive reasoning or deductive, it seemed highly unlikely to me that any meeting between Defoe and Selkirk ever took place. When I offered this conclusion to Professor Hans Turley of the University of Connecticut, an authority on Daniel Defoe whose acquaintance I later made, he wrote back as follows.

> *My own belief is that we shall never know if Defoe and Selkirk actually met. There are no notes left behind by either man. If you were to visit Bristol you would see that at least two taverns have plaques on them that say that the two men met in that particular tavern. Unfortunately there is no evidence that this is the case. Selkirk's story was, of course, well known to Defoe. Since both Dampier and Rogers wrote about discovering the castaway I think it is safe to imagine that Defoe read about Selkirk.*

Even so, there can be no doubt that the story of Selkirk's castaway experience gave off sparks in Defoe's imagination, as it stimulated him to write his first novel at the age of fifty-nine. The impact must have been enormous.

Selkirk's story burned itself into Defoe's memory and was transformed over time into an inner voice—a voice that called itself Robinson Crusoe and began one day to narrate an epic story.

That is how I see it.

Postscript

There was another legend. A tale of long ago, started by who knows whom. My pursuit of that will-o'-the-wisp landed me back in the city of Bristol.

King Street, which runs through the city center to the harbor on the River Avon, gave off an aura of yesteryear. Alongside the cobblestone road was an old wooden building, the kind you rarely see nowadays. On the signboard in front, along with the Welsh-sounding name "The Llandoger Trow," was the likeness of a ship. Once an inn, the place was now a bustling pub. According to legend, this was where, in the early 1700s, a journalist named Daniel Defoe sat down with Alexander Selkirk.

There wasn't a shred of evidence to support the theory. Yet as I sat at the counter sipping beer and looking around me, soaking in the rich, multilayered atmosphere of ages past, I felt a thrill as if I were listening to an ancient storyteller. It was the sensation of coming face to face with something unmistakably genuine.

Back in the eighteenth century when Defoe and Selkirk were alive, that pub was where the sailors and merchants of Bristol rubbed shoulders every day. The interior was scattered with ships' tackle, barrels, and carved figureheads, and I felt my imagination begin slowly to turn like the arms of a windmill in the breeze.

What deepens the mystery about Selkirk and Defoe is that Defoe left no notes about his inspiration for *Robinson Crusoe,* nor, as far as we know, did he talk to anyone about it. The origins of the novel are shrouded in obscurity.

Researchers seeking answers to the mystery have combed through "The Libraries of Daniel Defoe and Phillips Farewell," a catalog of books in Defoe's possession that provides clues to what he read and what may have influenced him.

And yet the catalog contains a fatal superfluity. After Defoe's death, his library passed into the hands of a London bookseller and was put up for sale November 15, 1731, at the Round Court in the Strand—but it was done so in combination with the library of one Dr. Phillips Farewell, an Anglican clergyman who predeceased Defoe by several months. The catalog of the sale listed all the books without specifying to which man's library they belonged, and to this day the two collections remain indistinguishable. In the strictest sense, therefore, the contents of Defoe's library are unknown. Of course the mingling of the two was deliberate, meant to ensure that the library of the relatively unknown Dr. Farewell sold at a high price. It's also conceivable that the dealer adjusted the contents of the sale for his own purposes. Some researchers therefore cast doubt on the general reliability of the catalog itself.

In any case, the catalog includes no writings with any bearing on Selkirk. Rescue accounts by Captain Woodes Rogers and Captain Edward Cooke are both missing, as is

Richard Steele's essay based on his interview with Selkirk. Not only is there no record of a personal meeting between Defoe and Selkirk—there's nothing to suggest that Defoe learned of the castaway's existence through his reading, either.

The deeper I went into the maze, the more twists and turns I encountered. The catalog seemed to indicate that Defoe had neither met Selkirk nor read Captain Woodes Rogers's account of the rescue. But was it true? As I searched through Defoe's writings, I came upon the following passage in *The Complete English Gentleman:*

> *He may go around the globe with Dampier and Rogers, and kno'*
> *a thousand times more in doing it than all those illiterate*
> *sailors.*[1]

William Dampier and Woodes Rogers were both sailors who circumnavigated the globe and published popular accounts of their travels upon returning home, becoming literary lions of the day. His dismissal of them as "illiterate" is in its own way revealing; by reading between the lines, we can infer that Defoe did in fact know of Selkirk's existence. His failure ever to mention Selkirk's name may then be seen as tacit indication of his awareness of the man.

And so the mystery deepened.

One day I went to the British Library and did a computer search for texts relating to Daniel Defoe. Records of Selkirk's movements during 1711–1718, the years of his repatriation, are scarce—but what of Defoe's movements during the same time span? I had a hunch it might be

---

1. Daniel Defoe, *The Complete English Gentleman* (London: David Nutt, 1890), p. 225.

worth a look. Just maybe, the two men's paths had crossed.

Finally, I came across one entry that grabbed my attention.

The Bristol Riot containing, 1. A Full and Particular Account of the Riot in General, with several Material Circumstances Preceding, and Contributing to it. 2. The whole proceedings relating to the Tryal of the Rioters, before Judge Powys, Judge Tracey, and Mr. Baron Price. By a Gentleman who attended the Commission. London: Printed for J. Roberts, near Oxford-Arms in Warwick-Lane, 1714.

According to the search list, the pamphlet was penned by Daniel Defoe. I homed in on the fact that it concerned a riot in Bristol in the year 1714. If the pamphlet was in fact Defoe's work, it would establish his presence in the city at a time when Alexander Selkirk might easily have still been around; in July 1713, Selkirk caused a violent altercation in Bristol, leaving for his hometown of Largo at some unknown date thereafter. The timing of the pamphlet seemed promising.

In my hunt for documentary confirmation of the legendary encounter in Bristol, the year 1714 might provide a point of contact between the two men. What if they were both in Bristol that year? The city is not large by any means. I kept on trying, but soon hit a new snag.

Since Defoe was a government spy, the authorship of his works isn't always clear. Most anonymous political pamphlets of his era are credited to him. Any study of Defoe's writing therefore has to begin with an examination of individual works to determine whether or not they are really his. I learned that the list of Defoe's writings I came up with in the British Library was based largely on "A

Checklist of the Writing of Daniel Defoe," published by John Robert Moore in 1960—a systematic study of all Defoe's putative writings, separating the genuine from the spurious. I lost no time in looking up "THE Bristol RIOT," and found this laconic comment: "Very probably, not quite certainly, Defoe's."

The comment was ambiguous, capable of interpretation either as support for the theory of Defoe authorship or as a disclaimer. There was still no way of knowing if Defoe had ever been in Bristol in 1714.

Just as I was wondering how to get a more definitive verdict, Dr. James Kelly at Worcester College, Oxford, a Defoe specialist, introduced me to a study negating the theory of Defoe authorship. In a scholarly essay entitled "Daniel Defoe, John Oldmixon and the Bristol Riot of 1714," Pat Rogers argues that people and events covered in the pamphlet have far less to do with Defoe's political opinions than with those of another contemporary pamphleteer named John Oldmixon. By a preponderance of circumstantial evidence, Rogers concludes that the pamphlet is unmistakably Oldmixon's work. And so the tempting theory of 1714 was reduced again to mere speculation.

Still, the Bristol angle remained viable. Selkirk lived in London for a while after his repatriation, leaving one other window of opportunity for a possible meeting with Defoe: the brief span from 1711 to 1712. What was the connection to Bristol then? For one thing, that was where Selkirk's rescuer, Captain Woodes Rogers, lived. To Selkirk, the man who rescued him from a lifetime of solitude was a savior, a kindly superior, and a fellow man of the sea with whom he could unwind. Once back in England, he must have looked up to the captain and relied on him in a special way. When he needed a sympathetic ear, it may have been to the captain that he turned, while drinking in The Llandoger Trow. Given Defoe's intimate association with merchants and seamen, there can be little doubt that he visited the pub, too. He would have gone there to drink ale and, perhaps, since it was then an inn, to change out of his travel clothes on the upper floor.

Then again, it was all conjecture. The truth remained an enigma.

I ordered another beer, then took out a book of old records that had never left my side during my travels and began leafing through it. The old accounts there mingled slowly with memories of my own long journey until the laughter and shouts of long-ago seamen and merchants seemed to rise up from the depths of my consciousness, filling my ears. Listening to that merry babble, I ran my eyes idly over the words on the pages, pausing at the name of Captain Woodes Rogers. Whatever became of him? I felt a surge of curiosity.

Following his dramatic rescue of the castaway, Rogers was appointed royal governor of the Bahamas, and in April 1718 he set sail from England, never to return. His life ended in Nassau in 1732, when he was fifty-three.

As I read the words, a chill went down my spine. Mixed in with the voices in the pub came the faint echo of a man's voice.

Coincidence? Just four months after Captain Rogers set sail for the last time in April 1718, in August of the same year Selkirk too set out on his fateful sea voyage in the *Weymouth*. No, it seemed no coincidence to me.

The hubbub gradually fell away, and I heard clearly what the voice was saying: *Selkirk followed Captain Rogers out to sea. In order to return to the island.*

Acknowledgments

Travel connects people, and my journey in quest of Robinson Crusoe brought me new friends around the world. Every time I met someone for the first time, I always began with the story of the real Crusoe. I was impressed that although just about everyone knew Defoe's *Robinson Crusoe*, few had any knowledge of the true story behind the literary masterpiece. Fortunately, my dream of going off in search of the real Robinson Crusoe attracted the interest of many people, who showered me with warm words of advice and encouragement. I was able to share my dream with many friends.

For their kind help in researching old documents, maps, navigational logs, and other relevant materials, I must thank librarians, curators and others at the Royal Geographical Society, the Explorers Club, the Public Record Office, the British Library, the Kenneth Spencer Research Library, Lennoxlove House, Fife Council, and the National Museums of Scotland. Jean and Jerry Parmer at Parmer Books in San Diego located a number of rare antique books for me. Clive Collins, his wife Keiko Collins, Roger Nixon, and Rika Takada provided kind assistance with old English or Spanish texts. Defoe specialists Dr. Hans Turley at the University of Connecticut and Dr. James Kelly at Worcester College, Oxford, provided invaluable hints and professional advice on literary research. Two descendants of Alexander Selkirk, Allan Jardine and the late Ivy Jardine, graciously met and talked with me, intensifying my interest in this captivating topic.

In Chile, Mauricio Calderon of the Corporation National Forestal not only gave me permission to conduct my research but also shared with me his precious knowledge of the natural history of the Juan Fernandez Islands.

Special thanks are due Dr. David Caldwell and his family; without David's extensive collaboration, this book would not exist.

Directly and indirectly, many people in Japan have also supported me in the publication of this book. I am deeply indebted to Tetsuya Terashima and Teruhisa Nakajima of Shinchosha Publishing House, which published the Japanese edition, as well as to Satoshi Sugita and his daughter Nami Sugita, Fumiko Yokoyama, Gavin Frew, and Stephen Forster.

After the successful publication of my book in Japan, I commissioned Juliet Winters Carpenter to translate it into English, and I would like to thank her for her fine translation and devoted work. Gratitude also goes to Ros Edwards, Helenka Fuglewicz, Jo McGarvey, and Julia Forrest, all members of the London-based literary agency Edwards Fuglewicz, to whom I sent the first few translated chapters. They offered to represent me and edited and sold my book internationally with tireless enthusiasm.

My grateful thanks of course go to Michael Dorr, for buying the American rights, to Ross Plotkin and Hector

DeJean of Cooper Square Press, and also to Julie Kirsch
for her conscientious copyediting and clear thinking.

DAISUKE TAKAHASHI
February 2002
Tokyo, Japan

Index

OTHER COOPER SQUARE PRESS TITLES OF INTEREST

THROUGH THE BRAZILIAN WILDERNESS
Theodore Roosevelt
New introduction by H. W.
  Brands
448 pp., 3 maps
0-8154-1095-6
$19.95

AFRICAN GAME TRAILS
An Account of the African
Wanderings of an American
Hunter-Naturalist
Theodore Roosevelt
New introduction by H. W.
  Brands
600 pp., 210 b/w illustrations
0-8154-1132-4
$22.95

THE DESERT AND THE SOWN
The Syrian Adventures of the
Female Lawrence of Arabia
Gertrude Bell
New introduction by Rosemary
  O'Brien
368 pp., 162 b/w photos
0-8154-1135-9
$19.95

EDGE OF THE JUNGLE
William Beebe
New introduction by Robert
  Finch
320 pp., 1 b/w photo
0-8154-1160-X
$17.95

STANLEY
The Making of an African
Explorer
Frank McLynn
424 pp., 19 b/w illustrations
0-8154-1167-7
$18.95

TUTANKHAMUN
The Untold Story
Thomas Hoving
408 pp., 43 b/w photos
0-8154-1186-3
$18.95

THE LIFE AND AFRICAN
EXPLORATIONS OF
LIVINGSTONE
Dr. David Livingstone
656 pp., 52 b/w line drawings and
maps
0-8154-1208-8
$22.95

MY ATTAINMENT OF THE
POLE
Frederick A. Cook
New introduction by Robert M.
  Bryce
680 pp., 45 b/w illustrations
0-8154-1137-5
$22.95

THE *KARLUK*'S LAST VOYAGE
An Epic of Death and Survival in
the Arctic, 1913–1916
Captain Robert A. Bartlett
New introduction by Edward E.
    Leslie
378 pp., 23 b/w photos, 3 maps
0-8154-1124-3
$18.95

EDGE OF THE WORLD: ROSS
ISLAND, ANTARCTICA
A Personal and Historical
Narrative of Exploration,
Adventure, Tragedy, and Survival
Charles Neider
with a new introduction
536 pp., 45 b/w photos, 15 maps
0-8154-1154-5
$19.95

ANTARCTICA
Firsthand Accounts of
Exploration and Endurance
Edited by Charles Neider
468 pp.
0-8154-1023-9
$18.95

CARRYING THE FIRE
An Astronaut's Journeys
Michael Collins
Foreword by Charles Lindbergh
512 pp., 32 pp. of b/w photos
0-8154-1028-6
$19.95

KILLER 'CANE
The Deadly Hurricane of 1928
Robert Mykle
268 pp., 22 b/w illustrations
0-8154-1207-X
$26.95 cl.

MAN AGAINST NATURE
Firsthand Accounts of Adventure
and Exploration
Edited by Charles Neider
512 pp.
0-8154-1040-9
$18.95

GREAT SHIPWRECKS AND
CASTAWAYS
Firsthand Accounts of Disasters at
Sea
Edited by Charles Neider
256 pp.
0-8154-1094-8
$16.95

THE FABULOUS INSECTS
Essays by the Foremost Nature
Writers
Edited by Charles Neider
288 pp.
0-8154-1100-6
$17.95

Available at bookstores; or call 1-800-462-6420
COOPER SQUARE PRESS
200 Park Avenue South
Suite 1109
New York, NY 10003